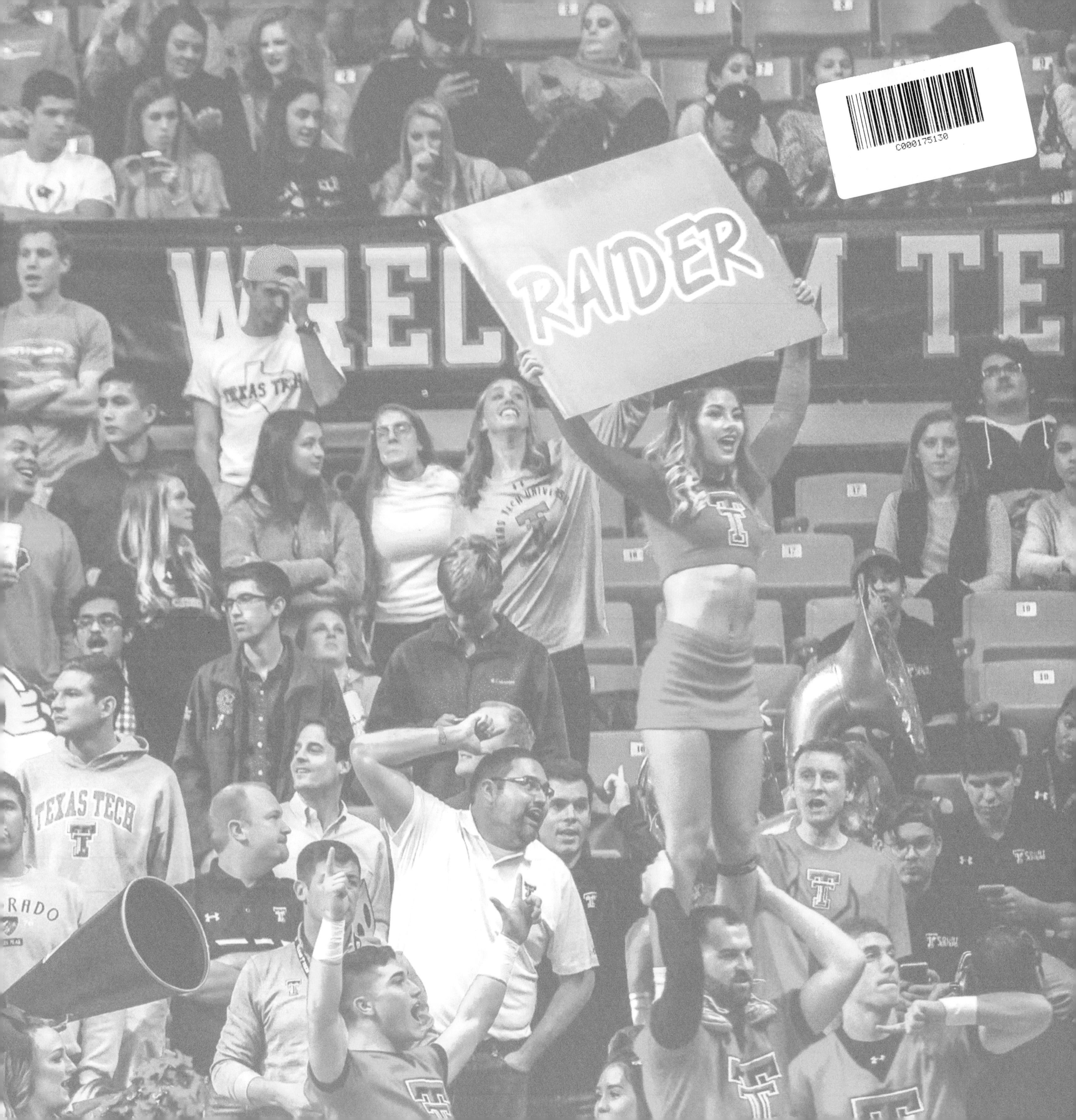
RAIDER
TEXAS TECH
TEXAS TECH

RAIDER POWER

RAIDER POWER

TEXAS TECH'S JOURNEY FROM UNRANKED TO THE FINAL FOUR

TEXAS TECH ATHLETICS

FOREWORD BY ANDY KATZ

TEXAS TECH UNIVERSITY PRESS · LUBBOCK, TEXAS

This book is typeset in Regular. The paper used in this book meets the minimum requirements of ANSI/NISO Z39.48-1992 (R1997). ∞

Text by Wes Bloomquist
Designed by Hannah Gaskamp
Cover photograph by Elise Bressler

Library of Congress Control Number: 2019946426

ISBN (leather): 978-1-68283-046-8
ISBN (cloth): 978-1-68283-047-5

Printed in China
19 20 21 22 23 24 25 26 27 / 9 8 7 6 5 4 3 2 1

Texas Tech University Press
Box 41037
Lubbock, Texas 79409-1037 USA
800.832.4042
ttup@ttu.edu
www.ttupress.org

Because of the commitment from the players and coaches to achieve historic accomplishments.

In honor of all former Red Raiders who helped establish the program.

For Corky.

CONTENTS

FOREWORD

FAMILY. FUN. FOCUS.

Those are the three words that I immediately think of when reminiscing about Texas Tech's historic 2018–19 season.

THE FAMILY

There was the hug, the one that I witnessed with Texas Tech coach Chris Beard and his daughters Avery, Ella, and Margo as the Red Raiders knocked off Michigan State to advance to the national championship. Chris bolted off the elevated court in Minneapolis and was nearly tackled by his three devoted girls racing to meet him halfway.

As a father, I loved seeing how doting Chris was with his daughters. Finding balance for a coach is incredibly difficult. The coaches who get it are usually the ones who can handle the stress of the job and probably are overall healthier. Finding time for family will always bring a sense of calm and peace. One benefit that isn't as widely known about progressing in the NCAA tournament is how much more time your family can be around. And Chris never lacked for including them, especially at the arena either on an off day or game day. It was clear that their presence put him at ease and allowed him never to get too overwhelmed by the enormity of what was occurring.

Beard's inclusion of his assistants like Mark Adams, whom he was constantly recognizing for his contributions, and reaching out to bring in Sean Sutton, showed how much Beard appreciated the profession and coaches who could complement him. Ego was never something that swallowed him.

There was the camaraderie among a collection of players who had come together for one common goal. A player from Italy. A native of the Dominican Republic. A transfer from South Dakota. And a star from Lubbock. All of them, every member of that locker room, seemed to fit each time I was around this crew. They merged their musical tastes. They never seemed to be rattled. They had a shared purpose.

THE FUN

There were the Fireside Chats. And I loved every one of them. I first caught wind of Beard's social media schtick earlier in the season. I immediately retweeted it and promoted it every time it was posted. Beard's delivery was perfect. His deadpan humor worked. And the guests were always in on the act.

We had a blast doing the chats on the road, from finding someone who could draw in the hallways in Anaheim, to using a laptop in a hotel conference room to project a makeshift fire, to Chris drawing a fire on a piece of paper that we taped behind us after the Red Raiders had reached the championship game.

Chris absolutely loved injecting levity into any situation, like texting me a picture of cheese and crackers before the national semifinal.

But embracing life wasn't just a part of this season. I'll never forget the looks on the faces of members of the TD Garden staff in Boston the previous year when the Red Raiders were blasting music that could be heard throughout the back hallways. If anyone was going to tell them to turn down the music, they weren't going to listen.

And even when they were on the eve of playing for the national title, going through their last practice of the season, the Red Raiders were on the court enjoying the music.

THE FOCUS

The Red Raiders knew who they were from day one. They were going to defend. They could shoot it better than most projected. And they were never, ever going to quit. Texas Tech's co-Big 12 title wasn't projected by anyone outside of its locker room. But of course the Red Raiders, despite having only one returning star in Jarrett Culver, quieted any of the critics (including me early).

Texas Tech was the hottest team going into the national title game. Prior to the overtime final, the Red Raiders hadn't really played a close game. Dispatching Michigan, Gonzaga, and Michigan State were three of the most impressive wins of the NCAA tournament. The Red Raiders had Virginia beat, too, before a series of events turned on them. Still, the run was remarkable, the style of play entertaining, and the resolve never in question.

Texas Tech arrived on the national stage as an easy team to embrace. The bandwagon may have new drivers each season, but getting on board won't be something anyone regrets.

Andy Katz

INTRODUCTION

THEY WERE STONE-FACED DREAMERS who began the year unranked and overlooked before fighting their way to play on the final Monday night of the season.

The 2018–19 Texas Tech Red Raiders made the NCAA National Championship Final as the best defensive team in the nation. They were tough and genuine, and they played with personality.

They believed in themselves when picked seventh of ten in the Big 12 preseason poll and when they were left completely off the national polls. Through successes and challenges, there was a fire that burned inside every member of the program. That figurative fire turned literal when the team set a stat sheet ablaze in a theater parking lot. Fire was also a place to connect with fans, through Coach Chris Beard's fireside chats.

Everything fueled the Red Raiders' desire to achieve their goals.

"All successful teams have an identity that has to be real," Texas Tech head coach Chris Beard said. "Our team had a street dog, underdog mentality all year. It started with our recruiting of players who were not highly ranked, but with guys that dreamed about winning the Big 12 and dreamed about playing on the biggest stage. We were disrespected by not being in the polls early in the season, and this team embraced it. With some teams you don't talk about polls, but we did with this team. With four seniors, we checked the polls every Monday and enjoyed people telling us what we couldn't do."

On the final Monday of the college basketball season, Texas Tech had gone from an afterthought in the preseason to playing Virginia for a national championship in front of 72,062 fans at U.S. Bank Stadium in Minneapolis, Minnesota.

"We told the guys in the summer that we felt like we had enough on our roster in terms of physical talent to win the Big 12 and play in the Final Four," Beard said.

"Yeah, he told us in the summer. I don't know if it was the first day, but it was early," recalled graduate transfer Matt Mooney. "He said that we have enough in this gym, in this locker room right here, to play on the final Monday night. He might be psychic because here we are on the final Monday night. We just believed him and believed in each other all year long."

"I thought three things would have to take place for those thoughts we had in the summer to come true," Beard said. "We had to be the best defensive team in college basketball, we had to be one of the toughest teams in college basketball physically and mentally, and we had to be the most together and connected team. I think ten months later when we made the Final Four, those things had come true."

Texas Tech finished the season with 31 wins—the most victories in the 94-year history of the program—won the Big 12 Conference regular-season championship, and progressed to the National Championship Final by advancing in the NCAA tournament with wins over Northern Kentucky, Buffalo, Michigan, Gonzaga, and Michigan State. On the final Monday night of the basketball season, Tech faced Virginia, a team ranked No. 5 in the preseason poll and No. 2 going into the postseason.

"The underdog mentality was real," Beard said. "There were people who thought Northern Kentucky was going to pull the upset; Buffalo was a team some had beating us and advancing; Michigan, Gonzaga, and Michigan State were all the favorite. We always respected our opponent, but we did so with a chip on our shoulder."

Make no mistake, though, you don't win one of the best conferences in the country or knock off a No. 1 seed without unbelievable talent. Texas Tech was led throughout the season by sophomores Jarrett Culver and Davide Moretti, and by the four-man senior class of Norense Odiase, Brandone Francis, Tariq Owens, and Matt Mooney.

Culver earned Big 12 Player of the Year (a first in program history) and was a Consensus All-American after leading the Red Raiders with 18.5 points, 6.4 rebounds, and 3.7 assists. A hometown kid from Lubbock, Culver scored a career-high 31 points against Iowa State to secure the regular-season title and came up big throughout the NCAA run, including dropping 29 on Northern Kentucky and 22 against Michigan. Mooney and Owens were graduate transfers who thrived in the culture from the beginning, and Odiase and Francis both used their Elite Eight experience from the previous year to provide key contributions and leadership throughout the season. Owens established a new program record with 92 blocked shots, while Mooney led the team with 70 steals. Moretti proved to be one of the top sharpshooters in the nation in his second year at Tech, making 49.8 percent of his shots from the field, shooting 45.9 on 3-pointers, and leading the nation at 92.4 percent at the free-throw line. His 50/50/90 percentage during conference play was the first for the Big 12.

Along with a rotation that included talented freshman Kyler Edwards and tough sophomore transfer Deshawn Corprew, the Red Raiders had the perfect mix of talent, edge, and commitment. Culver would score 26 points in the win over Kansas but gave credit to his teammates. Owens scored only two points against Northern Colorado but was the most enthusiastic player in the locker room, supporting the team that had won by 31. Mooney said he was terrible in the three-game losing streak and took accountability. Odiase ripped into the team after the loss at Duke that outsiders viewed as a moral victory and implemented a rule of no cellphones at night during road trips.

"Culture can be an overused word in sports these days, but it was so true with our team this year," Beard said. "Call it culture, chemistry, team unity, or anything else, the thing that made us special was that we played together every day as a team. The group was bigger than the individuals."

Their consistency and toughness were written into the stats. Tech was second in the nation by holding teams to a 37.0 shooting percentage for the season and third by limiting opponents to only 59.5 points per game. Whether it was a non-conference game, a Big 12 game, or in the NCAA tournament, the defensive intensity was always there.

"First year: 'process'"; second year: 'finish'; and then this year our theme was 'consistency'," Beard said. "It's not a fluff thing. It's something our teams commit to and live every day. We started thinking about that word during the summer and picked it at the retreat. Knowing that we had the talent to compete with every team in the country, we knew that one of the main things it was going to take was for us to be consistent every day in our preparation and every game. You can't have ups and downs to compete for championships. We went back to that throughout the season and kept that as a focus. Even when we were winning, that word took us back to our goal and kept us on track. Consistency was a word that was with us from our first practice to the final game of the basketball season."

Texas Tech would earn nine wins over teams that were ranked in the preseason poll, including a 29-point victory over Kansas that topped the initial ranking. The Red Raiders went 14–4 in conference play, starting the conference campaign with four straight wins over West Virginia, Kansas State, Oklahoma, and Texas. There was only one time all season with back-to-back losses, coming in a three-game stretch with a four-point home loss to Iowa State and then a pair of road losses at Kansas State and Baylor. After a non-conference win over Arkansas and a home win over TCU, the Red Raiders lost at Kansas before ripping off nine straight victories to secure a share of the conference title that was capped by an 80–73 win over Iowa State in Ames, Iowa.

Beard and his coaching staff of Mark Adams, Brian Burg, Max Lefevre, Sean Sutton, Glynn Cyprien, and Tim MacAllister built a championship culture of commitment to each other and the process. A team of graduate assistant coaches and student managers lived in the film room and in the gym, recording and analyzing every aspect to find an edge. When a player wanted to put up shots for two hours after practice or at 3 a.m., someone was there for him. In the weight room, strength coach John Reilly and assistant Brandon "Santa" Lee pushed the players and transformed their bodies and mentalities. There was no entitlement in the program, from the top with Beard through the senior class, the sophomore starters, and the student managers. Everyone was connected.

Sitting on the floor of the locker room following the 77–85 overtime loss to Virginia in the National Championship Final, Francis held hands with Owens and Mooney as the three cried together. In the locker room there was pain, with players either inconsolable or in stunned silence from the loss. It was heartbreaking for everyone: the players, coaches, managers, cheerleaders, lifelong fans, and people who fell in love with the team along the way.

"We put everything into this," said Francis to a group of reporters who had surrounded the players. "Nobody remembers second place."

"Nobody's going to remember second place," Owens echoed. "He's right. We've been the underdogs all year. Nobody's going to remember us."

They were wrong about that.

This book tells the story of how some unranked street dogs fought their way to a Big 12 championship and to the Final Four. The memories made during the Red Raider run to the NCAA National Championship Final will last forever.

Stay stone-faced and keep dreaming. There's still a lot more to come from the Red Raiders.

SEASON TIMELINE

REGULAR SEASON

NOVEMBER

vs. UTEP (Exhibition)
Nov 1
W, 85–61

vs. Incarnate Word
Nov 6
W, 87–37

HALL OF FAME CLASSIC TOURNAMENT

vs. Mississippi Valley State
Nov 9
W, 84–52

vs. Southeastern Louisiana
Nov 13
W, 59–40

vs. Southern California
Nov 19
W, 78–63

vs. Nebraska
Nov 20
W, 70–52

vs. Northern Colorado
Nov 24
W, 93–62

DECEMBER

HOOPHALL INVITATIONAL

vs. Memphis
Dec 1
W, 78–67

vs. Arkansas–Pine Bluff
Dec 5
W, 65–47

vs. Northwestern State
Dec 12
W, 79–44

vs. Abilene Christian
Dec 15
W, 82–48

vs. Duke
Dec 20
L, 58–69

vs. UTRGV
Dec 28
W, 71–46

JANUARY

at West Virginia
Jan 2
W, 62–59

vs. Kansas State
Jan 5
W, 63–57

vs. Oklahoma
Jan 8
W, 66–59

at Texas
Jan 12
W, 68–62

vs. Iowa State
Jan 16
L, 64–68

at Baylor
Jan 19
L, 62–73

at Kansas State
Jan 22
L, 45–58

vs. Arkansas
Jan 26
W, 67–64

vs. TCU
Jan 28
W, 84–65

FEBRUARY

at Kansas
Feb 2
L, 63–79

vs. West Virginia
Feb 4
W, 81–50

at Oklahoma
Feb 9
W, 66–54

at Oklahoma State
Feb 13
W, 78–50

vs. Baylor
Feb 16
W, 86–61

vs. Kansas
Feb 23
W, 91–62

vs. Oklahoma State
Feb 27
W, 84–80 (Overtime)

MARCH

at TCU
Mar 2
W, 81–66

vs. Texas
Mar 4
W, 70–51

at Iowa State
Mar 9
W, 80–73

BIG 12 TOURNAMENT

vs. West Virginia
Mar 14
L, 74–79

MARCH MADNESS

ROUND ONE

NORTHERN
KENTUCKY
MAR 22
W, 72–57

ROUND TWO

BUFFALO
MAR 24
W, 78–58

SWEET 16

MICHIGAN
MAR 28
W, 63–44

ELITE 8

GONZAGA
MAR 30
W, 75–69

FINAL FOUR

MICHIGAN STATE
APR 6
W, 61–51

CHAMPIONSHIP

VIRGINIA
APR 8
L, 77–85 (Overtime)

The Red Raiders huddle on the court prior to the start of a game at the United Supermarkets Arena.

PART I:
MEET THE RED RAIDERS

From the Coach Beard Glossary:

4:1 – The ratio of mental to physical. We talked a lot about being the most mentally tough team in the country. I thought our team embraced it as well as I've ever seen, and it's a huge reason we accomplished what we did.

The Secret's In The Dirt – We got this phrase from Jason Witten when he spoke to his team about putting in the day-to-day work. It really became a part of the culture during the season. No matter what happened throughout the season—success or setback—we took the mentality that it was time to get back to work. The secret for us was in the dirt.

TOGETHER in Tulsa, Oklahoma

TOGETHER in Anaheim, California

TOGETHER in Minneapolis, Minnesota

TOGETHER

THE RED RAIDERS bonded as a team on and off the court. That connection wasn't held just during games when the bright lights and cameras were on or when the pressure of winning a game was at its peak. For the team members, being together was a 24-hour commitment to each other from the time each player arrived on campus until the Raiders returned from Minnesota.

"Together" was a message that Coach Beard reinforced every day. Before practices in empty gyms throughout the country, the team ran the length of the court and back locked arm in arm. They shouted "together" as they made their way up and down the court, connected as one group, relying on every member of the program to stay united. It was a message underscoring that every player, every coach, every manager needed to be in unison for the team to progress.

TOGETHER at the Final Four

Texas Tech had a roster full of talented and dedicated players, but also mentors who brought unrivaled commitment and expertise. Like the players, the coaching staff and graduate assistants each had their own unique journeys that brought them together and meshed perfectly for the historic season that led to the Final Four. BELOW (from left) : Anthony Johnson, Elliott De Wit, Matt Temple, Darryl Dora, Ronald Ross, Gino Saucedo, and Casey Perrin.

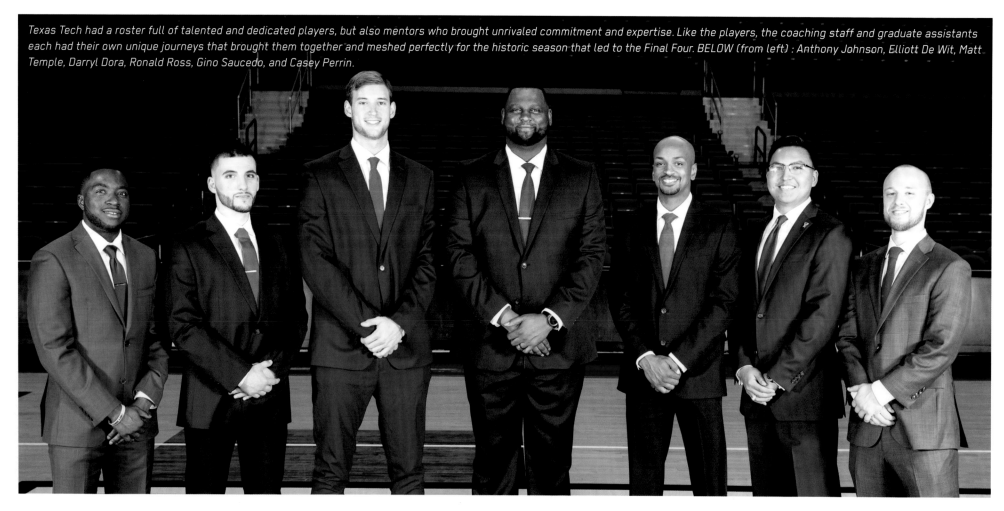

TOP (from left) Sean Sutton, Darryl Dora, Max Lefevre, Brian Burg, Chris Beard, Glynn Cyprien, Mark Adams, and Tim MacAllister.

Liz Cope, Avery Beard, Ella Beard, Margo Beard, and Taylor Sinclair pose for a photo during a practice at the NCAA Tournament in Tulsa, Oklahoma. Cope and Sinclair's work in the basketball office cannot be overstated and directly impacted winning on the court.

Brandone Francis shows off his dance moves at the Big 12 Media Day with teammates Norense Odiase and Jarrett Culver looking on. The Red Raiders spent the day in Kansas City promoting the program through interviews and video shoots before the start of the season.

TOP-20 SONGS FROM THE SEASON

Selected by Cooper "The Godfather" Anderson

1. Where Corn Don't Grow *(Travis Tritt)*

2. Down Below *(Roddy Rich)*

3. Old Town Road *(Lil Nas X)*

4. It's a Great Day to Be Alive *(Travis Tritt)*

5. Speed it Up *(Gunna)*

6. Adios Amigos *(Gary P. Nunn)*

7. Dreams and Nightmares *(Meek Mill)*

8. I Won't Back Down *(Tom Petty)*

9. Racks in the Middle *(Nipsey Hussle)*

10. Mamma Tried *(Merle Haggard)*

11. 2 of Amerikaz Most Wanted *(2Pac)*

12. God's Got a Blessing *(Norman Hutchins)*

13. Where My Dogs At *(Marsell Holden)*

14. I'm Gonna Be Somebody *(Travis Tritt)*

15. Juicy *(The Notorious B.I.G.)*

16. Superstition *(Stevie Wonder)*

17. Ye *(Burna Boy)*

18. One Shining Moment *(Luther Vandross)*

19. California Love *(2Pac featuring Dr. Dre)*

20. WIN *(Jay Rock)*

GROUNDBREAKING

DURING THE 2018–19 SEASON, Texas Tech would host a groundbreaking ceremony for the construction on the Dustin R. Womble Basketball Center in the City Bank Room of United Supermarkets Arena. This facility is another milestone for The Campaign for Fearless Champions.

"We look forward to breaking ground on what will be one of the premier basketball facilities in the country," Texas Tech Director of Athletics Kirby Hocutt said. Both the Texas Tech men's and women's basketball programs will move their day-to-day operations to the Womble Basketball Center following its completion. It will also house coaches' offices, athletic training facilities, and strength and conditioning areas for both programs.

JARRETT CULVER

JARRETT CULVER led Texas Tech in scoring, rebounding, and assists. He was also a hometown kid, a three-star recruit from Lubbock's Coronado High School.

Culver grew up in a family of athletes. His brother J.J. plays basketball at Wayland Baptist, and his brother Trey has the Texas Tech record for the high jump, 7 feet, 7 ¾ inches, which is the fourth highest all time in the NCAA.

After two seasons at Tech, Jarrett Culver made his own mark, finishing his collegiate career with 1,119 points. He was the first player in program history to surpass the 1,000-point milestone as a freshman/sophomore.

As a sophomore, Culver became the first Red Raider to ever win Big 12 Player of the Year. He earned Consensus All-American, selected by the Associated Press, National Association of Basketball Coaches (NABC), Sporting News, and United States Basketball Writers Association (USBWA) for the nation's most prestigious honors after leading the Red Raiders with 18.5 points, 6.4 rebounds, and 3.7 assists per game. Despite all his accomplishments, he always gave his teammates the credit and focused more on team goals.

"Our culture, hard work, and chemistry is what helped us win," said Culver, who helped Tech to a 58-17 record in his career. "We approached every day with a chip on our shoulder. We wanted to win, and we worked for everything we got."

Home games were a family affair for Culver. His father, Reverend Hiawatha Culver, would deliver the pregame prayer.

Culver announced his intentions to declare for the NBA Draft ten days after the national championship final: Culver was picked sixth overall. He was recognized as one of the most versatile players in college basketball.

Culver walks through the halls of the U.S. Bank Stadium at the Final Four.

"When talent intersects love of the game, special things happen," Beard said. "Jarrett worked on his craft. He came in here as a guy who could score. Two years later, he leaves as one of the best defensive players in college basketball."

In his sophomore season, Culver scored 20 or more points in 13 games with a career-high 31 coming against Iowa State in the regular-season finale to secure the regular-season championship. During the NCAA tournament run, he averaged 18.5 points per game including leading the team with 29 in the first-round matchup against Northern Kentucky and dropping 22 on Michigan in the Sweet 16.

"Basically since the first day that I recruited him until today, he's done everything that he said he would do," Beard said. "He's kept his word the entire way. He said he was going to be a team player, told me he was going to work hard every day, told me he was going to represent our program, told me he was going to be a leader and was going to let us coach him hard. Jarrett has always been so gracious and the most unselfish, best-player-type guy I've coached."

Norense Odiase takes a moment to focus before hitting a pair of free throws to give the Red Raiders a 68–65 lead with 22 seconds to play in the national championship game.

Odiase talks with members of the national media during a Final Four open-locker room session.

NORENSE ODIASE

NORENSE ODIASE stood in front of his teammates in their Madison Square Garden locker room after the team's loss to Duke and told them not to be satisfied. Simply playing a competitive game against Duke was not enough. Odiase knew his team was built to win.

Four months later, the day before the Red Raiders were to play Michigan State in the semifinals of the Final Four, the fifth-year senior stood in front of them, ticked off again. "You guys better not be buying into all that stuff. We haven't done anything yet."

The team had just gotten back to the hotel from enjoying a brief break that included eating yogurt and walking through a crowd of hundreds of Tech fans on the street who were congratulating them.

"We're here to win this," Odiase reiterated. "None of that matters right now. I'm mad we even saw that."

Throughout the season, Odiase was the one who voiced his opinion and kept his teammates focused on their goal. His season-high 14 points and 15 rebounds in the win over Buffalo was his on-court highlight, but his influence was crucial every minute of every day throughout the season.

"What made this year's team special was our unselfishness," he said. "We played for the names on the front of our jerseys, and not the back. Everyone respected and listened to one another."

Odiase went out as the winningest player in Texas Tech history.

Brandone Francis warms up prior to the start of the open practice at the Final Four in Minneapolis, Minnesota.

BRANDONE FRANCIS

BRANDONE FRANCIS was moments away from being off the team in his first season at Texas Tech. A native of the Dominican Republic, Francis started his collegiate career at Florida before transferring to Tech where in his first season he was moved into on-campus housing by Beard and challenged to become a better teammate, basketball player, and person. There was a contract signed between the two that laid out the expectations of what it would take for Francis to remain part of the program.

Francis lived up to that contract every day for the rest of his career as a Red Raider. In his final game, Francis led Texas Tech with 17 points after hitting three 3-pointers against Virginia. It was a career high, and it came when it mattered most.

"My best memory is playing in the national championship game," Francis said. "The last game of the season with a chance to win it all. I mean I never felt nothing greater than that. I gave my all, every bit of me, and I know my teammates did as well."

All season, Francis epitomized the team-first mentality that each Red Raider had to embrace. He was a reserve in 37 of 38 games and thrived in his role as the sixth man. He averaged 24.0 minutes and would contribute 6.5 points per game with eight contests in double digits. Francis hit 44 3-pointers during his senior season. Among his most memorable games was on Senior Night against Texas. With his mom and dad in the stands, Francis scored 12 points.

A month after the season, Francis graduated from Texas Tech University with a degree in human sciences.

Brandone Francis plays to the camera during a video shoot at the NCAA Final Four Media Day.

Brandone Francis celebrates with his mother, who had traveled from the Dominican Republic to be with her son on Senior Night, as Coach Beard looks on.

Matt Mooney celebrates as he walks on the court following Texas Tech's win over Michigan State at the Final Four. Mooney led the Red Raiders with 22 points in the game to help knock off the Spartans.

MATT MOONEY

MATT MOONEY arrived in Lubbock with one year of eligibility and with confidence in his decision to become a Red Raider. He trusted Chris Beard, the coaching staff, and his new teammates to give everything, just like he did.

Mooney was a pivotal player in the run to Texas Tech's first trip to the national championship final. A graduate transfer who had started his career at Air Force and South Dakota, Mooney had already established himself as a preeminent scorer in college basketball, but he had not advanced to the NCAA tournament. He wanted to play on the biggest stage.

Mooney and his mother met with more than 30 coaches as they decided where he would play during his final year of eligibility. Coach Beard flew through a snowstorm to make the recruiting visit. Mooney identified with Tech's program because it was full of under-recruited players coming out of high school and run by a coach who was working in Division II six years ago.

"I think we have a lot of guys who aren't five-star guys, coaching staff and Coach Beard who came from a mid-major and started out

coaching random teams and has worked his way up," said Mooney during a postseason press conference. "We try to embrace that, you know. We weren't the highest recruited guys, but that doesn't mean we can't compete with the best of the country. We just try to work at it every day."

Not just a worker, Mooney was a bona fide fighter. He boxed when he was at Air Force and would wrestle jovially with teammates and coaches in victorious locker rooms.

Mooney started all 38 games during the season and finished the year averaging 11.3 points, 3.3 assists, and 1.8 steals per game. He earned All-Big 12 Second-Team, All-Big 12 Newcomer, and All-Big 12 Defensive Team honors. His 70 steals throughout the season led the conference, and he had 16 games with four or more. He had a career-high eight assists in the NCAA first-round win over Northern Kentucky and then shined at the Final Four by hitting four 3-pointers in the 22-point performance against the Spartans.

Matt Mooney moves Texas Tech to the title game on the bracket in the locker room following a 22-point performance against Michigan State.

Texas Tech senior Tariq Owens looks to move the ball around the court in the Elite Eight matchup against Gonzaga in the NCAA Elite Eight in Anaheim, California.

TARIQ OWENS

TARIQ OWENS established himself as one of the most electric players in the nation on defense with his shot-blocking ability and offensively with thunderous dunks throughout the season. A graduate transfer who put his trust in Coach Beard and the Red Raider program for his final year of college basketball, Owens broke the program record with 92 blocked shots, which ranked sixth in the nation.

A Maryland native, Owens started his career at Tennessee and St. John's before transferring to Tech. Like Matt Mooney, he was hungry to play for a winner. Owens had never played on a team that had advanced to the NCAA tournament. Owens made this consideration his priority when considering schools in the recruitment process, and then set it as his driving force when he arrived in Lubbock.

Owens quickly became a leader on the team and in the locker room with his infectious personality, at practice with his determination, and in games with his two-way ability that shut down opponents defensively and offensively where he produced 16 double-digit scoring performances.

Owens shined in the tournament. One of his blocks against Gonzaga at the 3-point line when he saved the ball back in bounds was called "the play of the tournament" by analyst Reggie Miller on the telecast.

"Looking back on the season, the thing that made this team so special is how selfless the team was," Owens said. "It was always about we and not me. All we cared about was winning the next game on the schedule by any means necessary."

Owens was in Lubbock for only one season, but he will be remembered forever by fans who followed the team throughout and those who joined the journey in the Final Four. Owens was injured in the semifinal win over Michigan State in the Final Four but would fight through the pain to start against Virginia, where he played 22 minutes and contributed five rebounds and a blocked shot. He finished the year with a blocked shot in 37 of 38 games, and with an astonishing 270 blocks for his career.

Owens introduces himself to the Lubbock media after the first day of practice at the team's local media day.

Moretti gives high fives to teammates during the first day of practice.

DAVIDE MORETTI

DAVIDE MORETTI became the first player in Big 12 history to be a 50/50/90 (shooting, 3-pointers, free throws) shooter in conference play along with leading the nation by shooting 93.1 percent from the free-throw line throughout the season. A reserve in his freshman season, Moretti was one of three Red Raiders to start every game during their Final Four season.

Moretti came to Lubbock from Bologna, Italy, and hails from a basketball family. His father played professional basketball and is currently a head coach. During the postseason run, Moretti's mother, father, and brother would make a surprise visit before the Sweet 16 matchup against Michigan in Anaheim, California, where they would support him as the team made its run to the title game.

Moretti recorded 25 double-digit scoring performances, including a season-high 21 against Arkansas, and scored 20 against Oklahoma State and Iowa State.

Davide Moretti with his family in Anaheim, California.

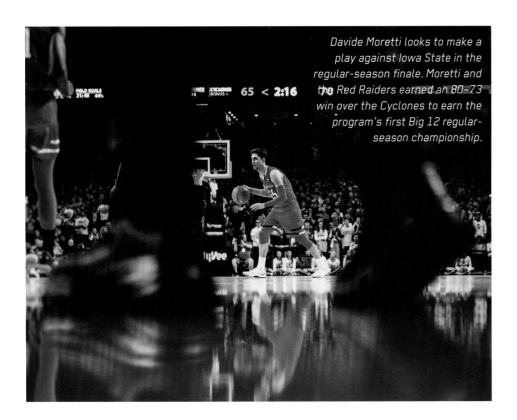

Davide Moretti looks to make a play against Iowa State in the regular-season finale. Moretti and the Red Raiders earned an 80-73 win over the Cyclones to earn the program's first Big 12 regular-season championship.

"Our expectations were to another level since day one, since our first non-conference game," Moretti said. "We knew we could win games by 30-plus points and when we didn't, we weren't even going to celebrate. We always wanted it more than anybody we faced."

Along with his on-court success, Moretti earned the NCAA Elite 90 Award as the student-athlete with the highest GPA at the Final Four and was a College Sports Information Directors of America (CoSIDA) Academic All-District and All-Big 12 Academic First-Team selection.

Moretti was second on the team in scoring throughout the season, averaging 11.5 points per game. Moretti completed the season shooting 97-for-105 at the free-throw line and led the Red Raiders with 73 3-pointers. He had a stretch during the season where he made at least one 3-pointer in 21 games and was 56-for-59 at the line during the final 17 games.

Deshawn Corprew makes his way to the basket in Tech's win over Kansas on Feb. 23, 2019, at the United Supermarkets Arena.

DESHAWN CORPREW

DESHAWN CORPREW won a national championship at South Plains College and would play for one in his first year at Texas Tech as a sophomore. After one of his best nights of the year, against Northern Colorado, Corprew spoke to the media and embraced the Texas Tech brawling attitude.

"I came here to play my role and be there for the team," Corprew said. "I just want to be a dog out there. I want to do the simple things. I want to go out there and do my best. I think I bring some energy, just like Brandone does. I think I bring a little toughness on the court, and people count on me to do the dirty work, like getting rebounds or making my open shots, defending the ball, and that's what I do for this team."

Corprew played valuable minutes all year and provided energy throughout. Ten points in the win over West Virginia helped start the nine-game winning streak, and twelve points at TCU were followed by seven points and six rebounds in the home finale against Texas.

A Norfolk, Virginia, native, he finished the season averaging 5.0 points and 3.3 rebounds per game with seven games in double-digit scoring. Corprew was fourth on the team in rebounding, completing the year with 87 on the defensive end and 36 offensive boards in 37 games played.

KYLER EDWARDS

Kyler Edwards has fun with a reporter during Tech's local media day prior to the start of the season.

One of those nights was the last one of the season. Edwards scored 12 points in the National Championship against Virginia.

All year the freshman served the Red Raiders as a talented young player coming in as a reserve and finished the year fifth on the team with 31 3-pointers, shooting 44.9 percent from beyond the arc. He made two 3-pointers in three NCAA tournament games and in eight games during the first season to help lead the team to the conference title.

He completed his first season in Lubbock averaging 5.5 points per game along with 42 assists and 23 steals.

KYLER EDWARDS didn't start a game all season but made an impact in all 38.

"We had a lot of great leadership from our upperclassmen and it showed throughout the season," Edwards said. "Coach Beard had a vision of shocking the world and every day he came to work and showed us how to execute that. The culture, work ethic, belief, talent, and mentality just intertwined together." Edwards said that Coach Beard gave him confidence.

"He tells me my time is going to be coming one day, any game. It was just my night tonight. It could have been anyone's night, but tonight was just my night. It just happened to be me tonight."

Kyler Edwards walks down the hallway of the United Supermarkets Arena to the court.

Texas Tech head coach Chris Beard celebrates a victory surrounded by his players and fans after a home win.

COACH BEARD

COACH CHRIS BEARD has led the Red Raiders to a 76–31 record over three seasons, including going 50–5 at home. Beard guided Tech to its first NCAA Elite Eight appearance in his second season (2017–18) before taking the team to the 2019 NCAA Championship Final. His 2018–19 Red Raiders won the program's first-ever Big 12 Championship and had the winningest season in program history with 31 victories. He was named the Associated Press National Coach of the Year and earned Big 12 Coach of the Year for the second straight season. Following the historic season, Beard signed a contract extension with Tech through the 2024–25 season.

"What Coach Beard, his staff, and the student–athletes have accomplished are not only historical moments in the university's history, but also tremendous sources of pride for Texas Tech University, Lubbock, and all Red Raiders," Texas Tech University President Lawrence Schovanec said.

Coach Beard noted, "Our fans were connected with this team. There was a personal connection they felt with our players and we were all on the journey together. I thought as the season went on our fans helped us more and more, culminating in the NCAA tournament. We had a home court advantage in the first two rounds in Tulsa, we had an unbelievable and humbling presence from our fans in Anaheim, and then in Minneapolis we arguably had more fans than any of the four teams there. We all knew somehow that we were on a special journey."

Chris Beard speaks with the media during a press conference after accepting the Associated Press National Coach of the Year award.

Chris Beard blows his whistle to give a breaking news alert at his Fireside Chat at Chimy's before the Red Raiders hosted Iowa State. The first-ever live edition of the Fireside Chat drew hundreds of fans and helped build on the enthusiasm for the program.

Beard posed for photos and signed autographs with the Red Raider fans after the event.

Coach Beard smiles while talking with fans after the live Fireside Chat.

Chris Beard and Jarrett Culver during a Fireside Chat.

The "fireside chats" that developed over the season were a way for Coach Beard to loosen up and connect with Tech students. The short segments were filmed in front of a digital fireplace: each time, Beard would give the schedule for the next home game, recommend music and food, and talk about whatever else occurred to him. He had numerous guests: players, assistant coaches, ESPN personalities, his daughters, and even Lubbock mayor Dan Pope. Highlights include a discussion of Wu-Tang Clan's "Protect Ya Neck," Whataburger, and Coach Beard's back tattoo.

The Fireside Chat was a fan favorite throughout the season and through the run in the NCAA Tournament, including this locker room edition after a practice in Tulsa, Oklahoma.

CHRIS LEVEL [TTSN]: "I was very fortunate to be around these guys all season long, and I realized very early on there was complete buy-in on every level of the team. Everyone enjoyed being around each other. I'm not sure people realize how much work went into each player's development or into building the chemistry they had. The payoff was a lengthy tournament run that brought a fan base together for a journey they will always remember."

SETH GREENBERG (ESPN): "Texas Tech has an elite basketball program that is bigger than just this team. Chris Beard has built a culture of ownership, passion, winning, and accountability. His energy is contagious, and his players not only believe and trust him but know how much he cares and is in it with them. This team is mentally and physically tough. They execute on both sides of the court. Texas Tech is here to stay."

Chris Beard leads the Red Raiders during a practice at the United Supermarkets Arena.

PART II: UNRANKED

From the Coach Beard Glossary:

Street Dogs – We pride ourselves on being the underdog and proving people wrong. Even though at the end we were ranked and competing for championships, we still never lost that street dog in each of us. We didn't have five-star recruits; we had a bunch of hungry, tough guys who fought for each other.

Don't Lose Your Chip – Our closed-door scrimmage against Houston was a great experience for our guys, and after the game Coach Kelvin Sampson came in and talked to our team. He told us to never lose our chip. He reminded us who we were. We're not North Carolina or Kansas with their tradition. We are Texas Tech. It was a message to never lose that edge you need to be great. We were unranked at that time. Coach Sampson reminded us to be true to who we are and to play with that chip on our shoulder.

Chris Beard talks with the team during their retreat in Stanton, Texas before the start of the season.

Norense Odiase struggles to stay on the rope during a challenge-course team experience, with teammates Kyler Edwards, Tariq Owens, and Brandone Francis trying to keep the group upright.

Jarrett Culver stands in front of his teammates during a truth-telling session talking about how he was promising to always be there for them. Culver came into the season with high expectations, but told his team that he didn't care about personal goals. He was there for them and would be no matter what.

RETREAT

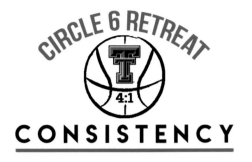

CIRCLE 6 RETREAT
CONSISTENCY

THE FIRST GAME on the schedule was November 6, but for the 2018-19 Texas Tech Red Raiders, the real season began on October 6, when Coach Beard took them on a retreat to the Circle 6 Ranch outside of Stanton, Texas.

The first AP rankings weren't out yet. That didn't matter on the retreat. The Red Raiders were a hundred miles away from Lubbock, forced to spend time getting to know each other, telling truths and forging connections. It was at the retreat that Beard and his assistants laid out the plan.

Every day matters, he told them, and "we have to do this together." He told them the season would be starting soon, that the trip to New York to play Duke was going to get there fast, that Big 12 play was right around the corner, and that before they knew it, the season would be over.

Norense Odiase, Brandone Francis, Tariq Owens, and Matt Mooney were starting their senior seasons, and Beard challenged each to be a leader. He told them that teams are only as good as their senior leadership and that he believed in them.

"I think everything started at the retreat where we laid everything out there as a team," Francis said. "We got closer and our unselfishness was a key to our success. That's when Coach started taking the lead and breaking everything down to the new guys and everyone around."

Beard praised each member of the program, while at the same time pointing out flaws. The team danced and sang at a late-night karaoke party, did trust-falls and ropes courses, and stood in front of each other during truth-telling sessions, opening up about past experiences that shaped who they were and what they were promising to bring to the team.

As Beard said, the next months raced by, whirling together into a lifetime of memories spent flying around the country, staying in fancy hotels, and playing games in the national spotlight. The weekend retreat was the moment that the team started forming their identity.

Texas Tech senior Tariq Owens high-fives his teammates during the first practice of the season.

FROM DAY ONE

Our expectations are pretty simple around here. We want to win every game on the schedule.

—Coach Beard

Texas Tech graduate transfer Tariq Owens throws down a one-handed dunk during the first day of practice. Owens would electrify Tech fans throughout the season. From the first day of practice to the final Monday night of the college basketball season, Owens gave the Red Raiders everything he had.

THE SEASON BEGINS

THE RED RAIDERS approached every game of the season as if it were the national championship final. They prepared for an exhibition game against University of Texas at El Paso and the opener against Incarnate Word with the same intensity and determination that they would five months later against Michigan State and Virginia at the Final Four.

This attitude was fueled by the preseason AP rankings, which were released October 22. While there were four Big 12 teams on the list, Texas Tech was nowhere to be found. It didn't matter. Those early season rankings were printed and one was ceremoniously burned in the parking lot.

Texas Tech respected and prepared for every opponent, using each game to get better, to instill a championship culture, and to become the toughest team in the country.

Deshawn Corprew looking down the court.

UTEP (Exhibition)
W, 85-61

Brandone Francis looks to move the ball around in the exhibition against UTEP.

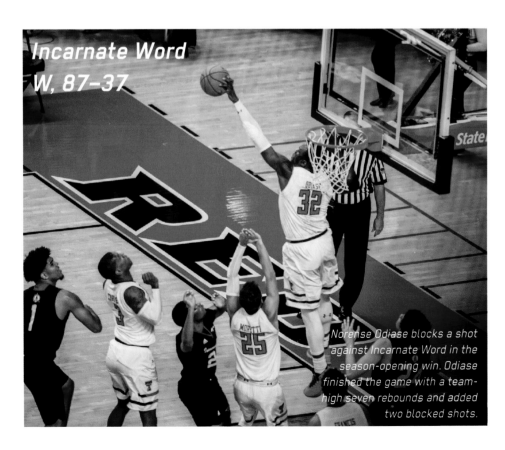

Incarnate Word
W, 87-37

Norense Odiase blocks a shot against Incarnate Word in the season-opening win. Odiase finished the game with a team-high seven rebounds and added two blocked shots.

Jarrett Culver puts up a jumper in the win over Southeastern Louisiana where he led the Red Raiders with 21 points.

Southeastern
Louisiana
W, 59-40

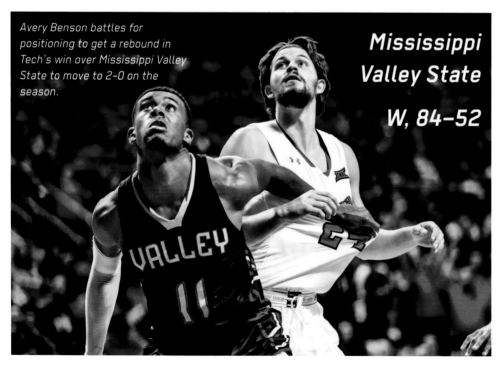

Avery Benson battles for positioning to get a rebound in Tech's win over Mississippi Valley State to move to 2-0 on the season.

Mississippi
Valley State

W, 84-52

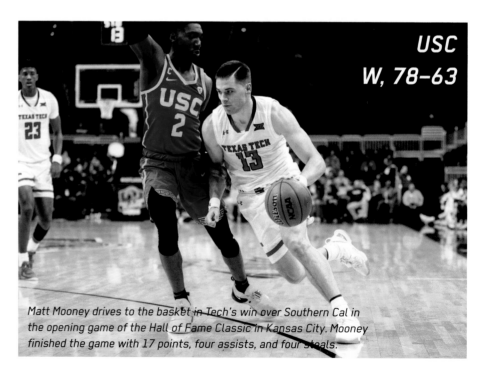

USC
W, 78-63

Matt Mooney drives to the basket in Tech's win over Southern Cal in the opening game of the Hall of Fame Classic in Kansas City. Mooney finished the game with 17 points, four assists, and four steals.

HALL OF FAME CLASSIC TOURNAMENT

Jarrett Culver led Texas Tech with 26 points in the 70-52 win over Nebraska to win the Hall of Fame Classic title in Kansas City. Culver hit nine shots in the game, including three 3-pointers for the Red Raiders.

Nebraska W, 70-52

Chris Beard and coaching staff members Tim MacAllister and Max Lefevre evaluate the situation during a game at the Hall of Fame Classic in Kansas City, Missouri.

JARRETT CULVER matched a career high with 26 points and Matt Mooney added 15 to help lead Texas Tech to the Hall of Fame Classic Championship title with a 70-52 win over No. 25 Nebraska on Tuesday, November 20 at the Sprint Center in Kansas City.

Tech had won the Hall of Fame Classic after earning wins over Mississippi Valley State and Southeastern Louisiana after the on-campus rounds of the event in Lubbock, and then a 78-63 victory over Southern Cal in the opening game in Kansas City.

The Red Raiders improved to 5-0 on the season and earned the tournament title after limiting the Cornhuskers (4-1) to 37 points below their season average. The team's defensive, street dog identity was beginning to take shape.

"We were really concerned with their offensive firepower and their ability to make the 3-point shot," said Texas Tech coach Chris Beard after the game. "I thought our guys were locked in tonight, especially on a one-day prep. I'm really proud of our team and it's evident that we have a veteran team with these four seniors. We embraced the preparation."

The Texas Tech Red Raiders may have passed their first test, but they were still unranked at the time they hoisted this trophy.

Chris Beard addresses the media during a press conference at the Hall of Fame Classic.

The Red Raiders talk with each other during a pregame huddle in the Sprint Center hallway prior to playing Nebraska in the Hall of Fame Classic championship game.

Chris Beard talks with the team on the court following their 70–52 win over Nebraska to earn the Hall of Fame Classic title in Kansas City, Missouri. The Red Raiders improved to 5–0 on the season with the victory and had earned their first trophy of the year.

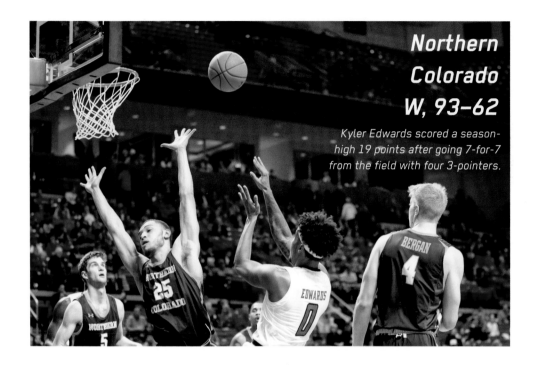

Northern Colorado
W, 93-62

Kyler Edwards scored a season-high 19 points after going 7-for-7 from the field with four 3-pointers.

Arkansas-Pine Bluff
W, 65-47

Brandone Francis and Tariq Owens rally the team from the sideline in a 65-47 win over Arkansas-Pine Bluff as the team improved to 8-0 on the season.

After the Hall of Fame Classic Tournament win, the Red Raiders continued to drive, winning against Northern Colorado, defeating Memphis in the Hoophall Invitational, and convincingly beating both Arkansas-Pine Bluff and Northwestern State. The Red Raiders' season record was now an impressive 9-0.

Memphis
W, 78-67

Tariq Owens recorded a double-double with 13 points and 11 rebounds along with setting a new Texas Tech single-game record with eight blocked shots.

Northwestern State
W, 79–44

Tariq Owens goes up for two of his 14 points in a 79–44 win over Northwestern State on Dec. 12, 2018 at the United Supermarkets Arena.

UTRGV
W, 71–46

Deshawn Corprew recorded a double-double with 13 points and 10 rebounds in the 71–46 win over UTRGV on Dec. 28, 2018. Corprew was 6-for-8 from the field and provided three steals in the victory.

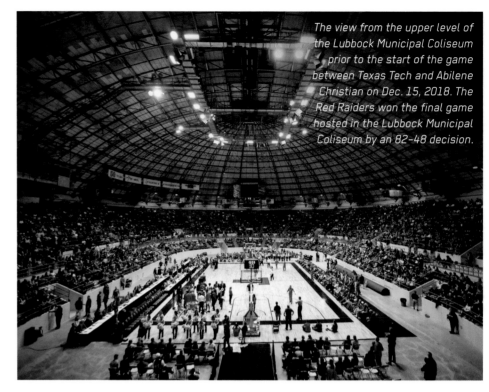

The view from the upper level of the Lubbock Municipal Coliseum prior to the start of the game between Texas Tech and Abilene Christian on Dec. 15, 2018. The Red Raiders won the final game hosted in the Lubbock Municipal Coliseum by an 82-48 decision.

Deshawn Corprew drives to the basket in Tech's win over Abilene Christian in the final game at the Lubbock Municipal Coliseum.

ONE LAST WIN IN THE COLISEUM

ABILENE CHRISTIAN UNIVERSITY [W, 82-48]

Jarrett Culver goes up for two of his team-leading 30 points in the win over Abilene Christian. Culver was 12-for-13 from the field and added seven rebounds in a performance that would earn him Big 12 Player of the Week honors.

THE RED RAIDERS played Abilene Christian University (ACU) in the final throwback game held in Lubbock Municipal Coliseum, affectionately known as "The Bubble." The Coliseum hosted its first game in 1956 against Kansas State and would be demolished in April 2019.

A Lubbock native playing in front of a sold-out Coliseum, Culver would add seven rebounds and four assists to his career-high 30 points.

"It was a very historic game for us," Culver said. "There's a lot of history behind it so we wanted to end it on a good night."

The Red Raiders improved to a 10-0 start to a season for the second time in program history. TTU shot 55.6 percent from the field in the game and limited ACU (9-2) to 28.3 percent shooting.

"The reason why we tried to play one of our best games this season tonight was to try to respect the people to have competed in this building," said Coach Beard.

Coach Beard celebrates a Red Raider basket in the final win at the Coliseum.

Jarrett Culver led Texas Tech with 25 points and added six rebounds against Duke.

SHOWDOWN AT MADISON SQUARE GARDEN

DUKE UNIVERSITY [L, 58-69]

TEXAS TECH LED BY two with six minutes remaining, but would see No. 2 Duke finish the game on a 16–3 run and take a 69–58 win over the Red Raiders on Thursday at a Madison Square Garden sellout.

It was their first regular season loss. "This says a lot about our team," Jarrett Culver said. "We have a lot of fight and heart on our team, a lot of great players that want to be coached. We see what we can be. We're not there yet, but we're going to learn from [tonight] and try to reach our potential."

"I think that the best thing about tonight was that we have a locker room full of guys who were disappointed," Coach Chris Beard added. "We expected to win the game. It's not arrogance, just a belief. We were right there. We get two wide-open 3s and two layups around the six- or seven-minute mark left in the game. I thought if we could've gotten those, the momentum would've swung a little bit. But, this is what Duke does. They just know how to win. We have a lot of respect for their program."

Culver led the Red Raiders with 25 points and had four assists and six rebounds, while Norense Odiase had seven rebounds and seven points. Texas Tech led by as many as seven in the second half and had a 55–53 lead on a layup by Matt Mooney before Duke went on a 7–0 run to take a 60–55 lead and then a 9–1 run to end the game.

Culver had come out as a superstar on the biggest stage of the season so far.

"He's one of the best guys in college basketball," Beard said. "The secret is out. Jarrett Culver is a great player. And what makes him really special is the kind of person he is, his character. He's the real deal. He's going to kill you in one-on-one at 10:30 a.m. on Sunday, then he's going to help you go to church at 11:15. He's special."

Mooney finished the game with seven points, five rebounds, and two steals, while Tariq Owens and Kyler Edwards had six points each. Edwards was 3-for-6 shooting on the night, to lead the bench for the Red Raiders who would finish the game shooting 44.0 percent but with a season-high 24 turnovers.

"We just had a lot of uncharacteristic, unforced turnovers," Beard said. "So that's the stuff we have to clean up. But, give Duke credit."

Zion Williamson led the Blue Devils with 17 points and 13 rebounds for the double-double, while RJ Barrett had 16 points and six assists.

"It was a great experience," Culver said. "We played a great team out there in Duke. We're going to learn from it."

The Red Raiders pose for a photo in the New York City subway on their way to see The Lion King on Broadway.

From left, Jarrett Culver, Malik Ondigo, Brandone Francis, and Davide Moretti pose for a photo in the New York City subway.

After each practice on the road there was a one-on-one game between coaching staff members and others who were on the trip. At Rucker Park in New York, Darryl Dora puts up a hook shot against Matt Temple in a matchup of former Red Raider players who were a part of the coaching staff.

After the loss to Duke, the Red Raiders came back and won at home against University of Texas at Rio Grande Valley.

The non-conference schedule established a few things about the Red Raiders. It showed that the team had a go-to player in Culver, graduate transfers Tariq Owens and Matt Mooney had made good choices in Tech, Moretti was ready to take a huge sophomore-season leap, and the experience Norense Odiase and Brandone Francis had gained throughout their careers was going to be beneficial for senior leadership.

While Jarrett Culver had introduced himself to the nation as a freshman, he solidified his presence as one of the top players in the country throughout the non-conference schedule. Culver led Tech in scoring in 11 of 13 games during that part of the season's fight. The team was coming together.

"I thought above everything, we just stayed the course," Texas Tech coach Chris Beard said.

By this time, the guys in the locker room weren't the only people who believed in the team. Even with the loss against Duke at Madison Square Garden, Texas Tech was entering the conference part of the season having gone from unranked and unnoticed to number 11 in the country.

HOLLY ROWE (ESPN): "The Red Raider passion is real. From the first game I covered at Madison Square Garden vs Duke, I could feel the passion and dedication from the fans for this special team. With that kind of combination of support and unity on and off the court, the team success didn't surprise me at all. I am just grateful I got to witness so much of it firsthand. What a wonderful season."

FRAN FRASCHILLA (ESPN): "Texas Tech Basketball has had pockets of brilliance through the years, but Chris Beard has turned the Red Raiders into a national program in a short period of time. I've seen few teams commit to success on a daily basis like this one from the head coach on down and it showed this season. I sense that this might only be the beginning."

The Red Raiders celebrate winning the Big 12 regular-season championship after an 80–73 win over Iowa State on March 9, 2019 in Ames, Iowa.

PART III:
BIG 12 CHAMPIONS

From the Coach Beard Glossary:

Truth Tellers – It sounds obvious, but we pride ourselves in telling every player and every coach the truth all the time. We don't play mind games. We don't have time for fluff. We weren't going to feed into egos by trying to build someone up too much. We weren't going to shy away from coaching them tough. It helped establish a culture and build relationships.

Get In The Fight – You have to put yourself in the fights to win them. The perennial powers go about a season by winning parts of the season that progress to the ultimate goal.

Stone-Faced – I got this when I was coaching the Swiss National Team and we played Russia. I had never seen anything like it. They were tough with zero emotion. They would make a great play and went on to the next play. They hit some adversity and moved right on. No emotion.

West Virginia
W, 62–59

Matt Mooney and Davide Moretti help Brandone Francis up from the court in the Big 12 opener at West Virginia.

Davide Moretti goes up for two of his team-leading 19 points in the 63-57 win over Kansas State on Jan. 5, 2019. Moretti hit three 3-pointers and was 7-for-11 from the field to help the Red Raiders improve to 2-0 in conference play.

Kansas State
W, 63–57

Norense Odiase battles for the ball in the hard-fought win against West Virginia.

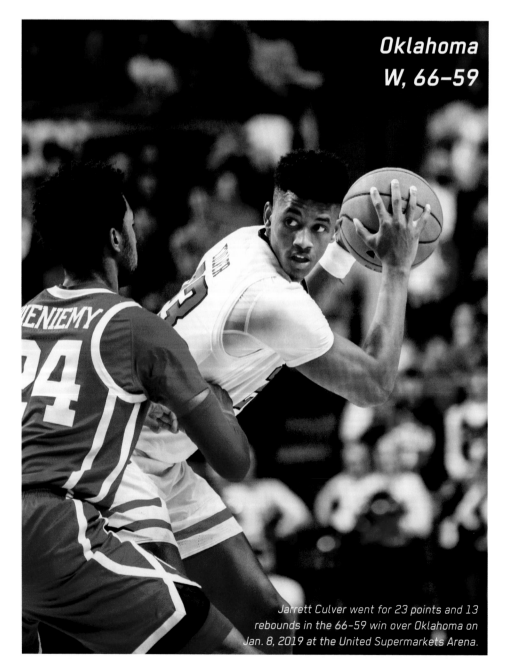

Oklahoma
W, 66–59

Jarrett Culver went for 23 points and 13 rebounds in the 66–59 win over Oklahoma on Jan. 8, 2019 at the United Supermarkets Arena.

CONFERENCE PLAY

Brandone Francis looks to make a move to the basket in the 66-59 win over Oklahoma to move to 3-0 in conference play. Tech limited the Sooners to 32.3 percent shooting at the United Supermarkets Arena.

AFTER THE RAIDERS' first win of conference play, Coach Beard said that the always competitive Big 12 was "an 18-round fight."

Texas Tech earned its first-ever win at West Virginia with a 62-59 victory over the Mountaineers in its Big 12 opener on January 2, 2019.

The Red Raiders were 0-6 all-time in Morgantown coming into the game and were limited to 20 points in the first half before making a comeback and earning the win over the Mountaineers.

"I'm just really happy for our players," said Chris Beard after the win. "The main reason is that nobody respects West Virginia basketball or Coach [Bob] Huggins more than I do and more than we do."

Jarrett Culver scored all of his 18 points in the second half after shooting 6-for-8 from the field and 6-for-6 at the free-throw line. Davide Moretti added 14 points, including a 3-pointer to give the Red Raiders a 55-54 lead with 2:09 remaining before Culver made

a jumper and four free throws to secure the road to victory to open conference play.

West Virginia led 22-14 with 3:33 remaining in the first half before the Red Raiders went on a 17-0 run.

Matt Mooney went for 14 points after knocking down five shots from the field and four from the free-throw line, while Moretti finished with 12 after hitting two 3-pointers. Brandone Francis scored eight for the second straight game and added four rebounds, and Norense Odiase and Tariq Owens each had four points. Texas Tech finished the game shooting 21-for-55 (38.2 percent) while West Virginia shot 41.9 percent from the field and was limited to 5-for-19 on 3-pointers. The Red Raiders were 17-for-24 from the free-throw line and the Mountaineers were at 18-for-32 in a game where Owens, Odiase, and Kyler Edwards each fouled out and Culver had four fouls.

Following the West Virginia win, huge crowds at the United Supermarkets Arena saw their Red Raiders score key victories against Kansas State and Oklahoma. Texas Tech improved to 3-0 in Big 12 play and 10-0 at home this season.

"I thought we showed grit," Chris Beard said. "We weren't playing our best at one point, but we hung in there. We just held on, and that's a good thing in the game of basketball. If you can hold that threshold you're doing good."

The street dogs had held all their conference opponents to under 70 points so far as their smothering defense continued to be the story of the season.

Matt Mooney makes a layup in a 22-point performance to help lead the Red Raiders to a win over Texas in Austin. The Red Raiders improved to 15-1 on the season and to 4-0 in Big 12 play with the victory. Mooney was 8-for-10 from the field, including knocking down three 3-pointers.

HISTORIC AUSTIN WIN
UNIVERSITY OF TEXAS [W, 68-62]

Texas Tech earned its first win at Texas since 1996 and enjoyed the victory as a team together with a postgame celebration in the locker room.

Tariq Owens throws down a dunk on the Longhorns for two of his 12 points in the win. Owens led the Red Raiders with four blocked shots and was 4-for-5 from the field and 4-for-4 at the free-throw line in the historic TTU win.

TEXAS TECH'S LAST WIN in Austin had been on February 24, 1996, back in the last days of the Southwest Conference.

Matt Mooney scored a season-high 22 points and Jarrett Culver went for 14 points and nine rebounds to lead the No. 8 Red Raiders to a 68-62 win over Texas. Texas Tech thereby ended a stretch of 22 straight Big 12 road losses to the Longhorns and for only the second time in program history improved to 4-0 in Big 12 play.

"The main reason I'm happy for our guys is because I think we just beat a really good team that is going to be a part of the fight," Texas Tech coach Chris Beard said. "We are a defensive team. That's our identity. Teams like Texas make it look like you can't play defense from time to time. I thought our guys were dialed in for most of the game."

The Red Raiders (15-1, 4-0 Big 12) finished the game shooting 44.4 percent from the field with five second-half 3-pointers and were 13-for-17 at the free throw line. Texas was 23-for-57 from the field and was only the third team this season to shoot over 40 percent against the Red Raider defense, which held teams to 33.8 percent shooting for the season.

Fans celebrate a win at the United Supermarkets Arena where the Red Raiders finished 17-1 at home for the second straight season.

Kansas State
L, 45–58

Texas Tech dropped its third straight game with a 45–58 loss to Kansas State on Jan. 22, 2019 in Manhattan, Kansas. The Red Raiders, who had opened Big 12 play with four straight wins, were now 4–3 in conference play going into a matchup against Arkansas in the Big 12/SEC Challenge at the United Supermarkets Arena.

Iowa State
L, 64–68

"THE SKID"

Tariq Owens looks to make a move to the basket against Baylor on Jan. 19, 2019 at the Ferrell Center in Waco. Owens finished the game with eight points and six rebounds, but the Red Raiders would fall 62-73 to the Bears to fall to 4-2 in conference play.

"ADVERSITY IS COMING. How will you respond?" This refrain was repeated over and over by Coach Beard during summer workouts, the team retreat, in preseason practices, and even when they ran off 10 straight wins to start the season.

Playing in the Big 12 is a grind, and Coach Beard told his team that the road to a championship was not going to be easy.

After a 10-0 start to the season and beginning Big 12 play at 4-0, the Red Raiders would stare adversity in the face for the first time with three straight losses to Iowa State, Kansas State, and Baylor. For the remainder of the season, Beard would answer questions about the "losing streak" and would talk about how it made the team stronger, but also that it was simply a reality when playing in the Big 12. Losses are going to come, he'd say, but it's how you respond to them that determines who wins the league.

The Red Raiders had forced themselves into the national conversation, climbing up the AP rankings to No. 8, having been unranked to start the year. They had fought their way up as underdogs; now they needed to learn to establish themselves at the top.

"We are just going to continue to fight and scrap," Beard said. "These games are tough to win. Today I'm just disappointed. I thought we beat ourselves in a lot of ways."

Adversity had hit, but the Red Raiders were ready to respond.

Arkansas
W, 67–64

Davide Moretti led Tech with 21 points after going 6-for-9 from the field and hitting three 3-pointers. Moretti also hit six free throws as the Red Raiders snapped a three-game losing streak with the win over Arkansas.

After the three-game losing streak, Texas Tech played its final non-conference game of the year by hosting Arkansas on January 26, 2019, and regained a bit of their mojo. Tech's win was its 47th straight non-conference home win and gave the Red Raiders a 40–39 in their all-time series with the Razorbacks that started in 1942.

Davide Moretti scored a career-high 21 points and Jarrett Culver added four 3-pointers to help lead No. 14 Texas Tech to the 67–64 Big 12/SEC Challenge win over the Razorbacks at the United Supermarkets Arena. The win helped the Big 12 to a 6-4 record in the challenge and snapped a three-game losing streak by the Red Raiders.

Said Beard: "On a night where we didn't play our best, I think you have to give Arkansas a lot of credit, but I do think our guys showed a lot of grit to come back after being down at half time and finding a way to win, when it really wasn't our best night."

They kept their momentum going against TCU, scoring more points that night than at any previous conference game. The Red Raiders would struggle against Kansas, falling 63–79 at Allen Fieldhouse, but they were ready to make their run.

Jarrett Culver dribbles the ball up the court for the Red Raiders versus Arkansas. Culver hit four 3-pointers in the win and finished with 15 points.

TCU
W, 84–65

Matt Mooney went for 18 points and also added five assists to help lead the Red Raiders to an 84–65 win over TCU on Jan. 28, 2019 at the United Supermarkets Arena. The win snapped a three-game Big 12 losing streak and took Tech to 17-4 on the season and to 5-3 in conference play.

Kansas
L, 63–79

Tariq Owens throws down a dunk in a 63-79 loss at Kansas as the Red Raiders fell to 5-4 in conference play. Owens recorded a double-double in the loss with 12 points and 10 rebounds to go along with three blocks.

Norense Odiase looks for options against Kansas on Feb. 2, 2019 in Lawrence, Kansas. The Red Raiders lost 63-79 at the Allen Fieldhouse in what would be their final loss of the regular season.

West Virginia
W, 81–50

Davide Moretti dribbles the ball up the court in the 81–50 win over West Virginia on Feb. 4, 2019 at the United Supermarkets Arena. Moretti finished the game with 11 points and four assists and helped the Red Raiders limit West Virginia to 9-for-39 shooting (23.1 percent) in the game.

Brandone Francis puts up a shot in a 31-point win by the Red Raiders over West Virginia in Lubbock. Francis led Texas Tech with 16 points in the win after going 7-for-10 from the field with two 3-pointers against the Mountaineers.

"THE STREAK"

HAVING SKIDDED BACK ten spots in the AP rankings to number 18, Texas Tech was 5–4 in conference play with nine games remaining on the schedule. They were starting to be written off in the Big 12—exactly the mentality that had fueled the Red Raiders so far.

They responded in a big way by winning every single game and earning the Big 12 title that looked elusive after the loss to Kansas.

The first of those nine wins was against West Virginia in a home game that was featured on ESPN's Big Monday. Tech had already knocked off the Mountaineers once with a 62–59 win, but this time the street dogs made a statement with an 81–50 victory, limiting the Mountaineers to 23.1 percent shooting and forcing 26 turnovers.

The Red Raiders set a new Big 12 record for fewest field goals allowed in a conference game.

Coach Beard in his postgame press conference said, "We responded and we told each other the truth. I think you have to give our players credit for responding when our backs were against the wall. I was not pleased in the way we played against Kansas. All you can do is respond. Tonight I thought we played much better."

Brandone Francis led Texas Tech with a season–high 16 points in a game where nine Red Raiders scored.

"I was a little more focused today," Francis said. "I went out there and played with a chip on my shoulder with something to prove. I talked to my mom today. I had it in my mind, and I just went out there with a chip on my shoulder thinking about my family."

BUILDING MOMENTUM IN NORMAN

OKLAHOMA [W, 66-54]

TEXAS TECH IMPROVED to 7-4 in conference play with senior Norense Odiase securing 11 rebounds, freshman Kyler Edwards recording a career-high six assists, and four Red Raiders scoring in double figures in a 66-54 road win over Oklahoma on February 9, 2019, at the Lloyd Noble Center.

Tech limited the Sooners to 36.2 percent shooting, owning the rebounding advantage and matching a season best with 10 3-pointers.

Davide Moretti led the Red Raiders with 14 points after hitting four shots from the field and going 4-for-4 at the free-throw line, while Jarrett Culver had 13 points and Matt Mooney and Brandone Francis had 11 each. Tariq Owens recorded his sixth game with four or more blocks.

Jarrett Culver lays in two of his 13 points in a 66-54 win over Oklahoma on Feb. 9, 2019 at the Lloyd Noble Center in Norman, Oklahoma.

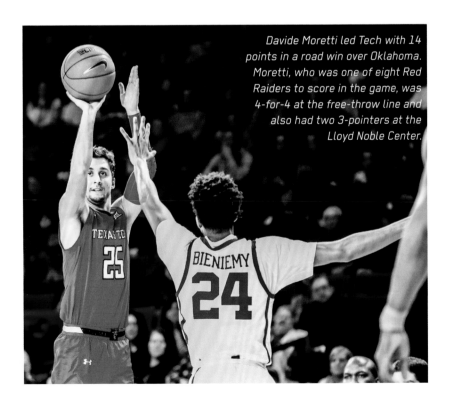

Davide Moretti led Tech with 14 points in a road win over Oklahoma. Moretti, who was one of eight Red Raiders to score in the game, was 4-for-4 at the free-throw line and also had two 3-pointers at the Lloyd Noble Center.

Matt Mooney was on fire in Stillwater, Oklahoma on Feb. 13, 2019 where he was 5-for-5 from beyond the arc. Mooney finished the game with 15 points, and Jarrett Culver led the team with 19 points as the Red Raiders improved to 20-5 on the season.

SHINING IN STILLWATER

OKLAHOMA STATE (W, 78-50)

MATT MOONEY made five 3-pointers, Davide Moretti had a career-high eight assists, and the No. 15 Red Raiders hit a season-high 12 shots from beyond the arc in a 78-50 Big 12 Conference victory over Oklahoma State on February 13, 2019, at the Gallagher-Iba Arena.

The Red Raiders won their third straight game after going up 21 points at halftime and ran away with the game in the second half by going on a 15-0 run to start the half.

The defense limited the Cowboys to 36.7 percent shooting, forced 14 turnovers, and led 62-25 with 13:37 remaining. The Red Raiders committed only eight turnovers in the game and shot over 50 percent for the ninth time, limiting their opponents to under 40 percent in 16 of 25 games.

"Once we start making shots, we're really hard to guard," Mooney said. "We were able to get the ball inside and spray it around. We got hot tonight and played well offensively."

Matt Mooney gathers himself in the lane in a 78-50 win over Oklahoma State on Feb. 13, 2019 in Stillwater, Oklahoma. Mooney finished the game with 15 points after hitting five 3-pointers for the Red Raiders.

BACK IN THE FIGHT

BAYLOR (W, 86-61)

NOW RANKED No. 15, the Red Raiders (21-5, 9-4 Big 12) extended their conference winning streak to four and improved to 14-1 on their home court by avenging their loss to the Bears earlier in the season in Waco.

"Our objective has always been to be a part of the fight," said Coach Beard in the postgame press conference. "A lot of people thought that we weren't going to be able to get back into the fight. You got to give those seniors credit. It starts with Brandone Francis and Norense Odiase, returners that believed. Then there's Tariq Owens and Matt Mooney, came to this program to make an imprint from Day 1 and they have. There's a lot of basketball left, but I think it's an accurate statement to say Texas Tech is a part of the fight right now with a few weeks left. We're in contention for the conference championship and that's our goal."

Texas Tech would limit its turnovers to only nine, including zero from Mooney and Moretti. The Red Raiders shot 40.7 percent from the field and limited Baylor to only 34.7 percent shooting.

Culver led the Red Raiders with his 18 points by hitting three 3-pointers and going 7-for-8 at the free-throw line. He would add four assists and was averaging 17.7 points, 6.3 rebounds, and 3.7 assists per game at that point in the season. Moretti stayed hot from beyond the arc, going 4-for-8 and finishing with 17 points. Owens made up the third Red Raider to provide double-figure scoring by contributing 11 points for the second straight game.

Norense Odiase puts up a shot in the 86-61 win over Baylor. The Red Raiders moved to 9-4 in conference play with the victory.

TECH TROUNCES KANSAS

KANSAS [W, 91-62]

EVERYTHING WORKED for the Red Raiders against No. 12 University of Kansas (KU) in what was arguably their masterpiece victory. Tech led by 25 points at halftime after knocking down nine 3-pointers and put the game away in the second half by shooting 68 percent from the field, including going 7-for-11 from beyond the arc. In all, Tech matched a program record by hitting 16 3-pointers.

"If we shoot the ball like this, we could beat anybody in the country," Coach Beard said. "Every guy on our team tonight shot 50 percent or higher, we had a low turnover game, we out-rebounded them, and tonight we played as well as we could."

The win over Kansas evened the season series with the Jayhawks, always a point of pride for any Big 12 team.

Tech finished the 29-point win with four players scoring in double figures. Culver made 10 field goals, including three 3-pointers, bringing his career total points to 901. Matt Mooney and Davide Moretti also had three 3-pointers in the game, and Odiase added eight points and matched his career high with the 13 rebounds. Tariq Owens added 10 points and kept his streak of blocked shots going with one in the game.

Brandone Francis also made three 3-pointers and finished with nine points, while Kyler Edwards and Deshawn Corprew hit two each. Edwards finished with eight points, while Corprew contributed six after going 2-for-2 from beyond the arc to give the Red Raiders six players who made two or more 3-pointers in the game.

"It's always good to see the ball go in as much work as you put in," Culver said. "Everybody in our program works hard, and we work hard every day. So, just to see the results is always good."

Jarrett Culver goes up for a dunk in a 29-point win over Kansas in Lubbock. Culver led the Red Raiders with 26 points after hitting 10 shots, including three 3-pointers.

Tech students, who wore white as part of a Game of Thrones themed whiteout, arrived hours before the doors were open and were loud throughout the game.

Kyler Edwards, who had eight points in the win, stays focused on the defensive end of the court in the victory over Kansas. The Red Raiders limited the Jayhawks to 20 points in the first half and improved to 10-4 in conference play with the victory.

Davide Moretti enjoys the postgame celebration on the court with fans after Tech's win over the Jayhawks.

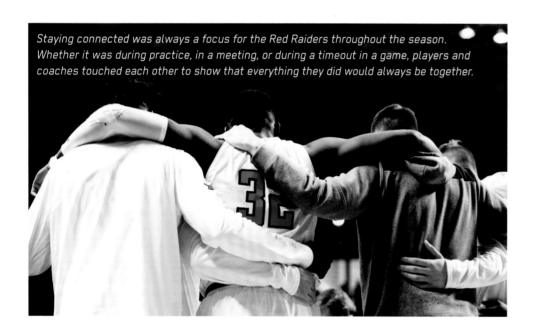

Davide Moretti was 12-for-12 at the free-throw line and led the Red Raiders with 20 points in an 84–80 overtime win over Oklahoma State at the United Supermarkets Arena.

Staying connected was always a focus for the Red Raiders throughout the season. Whether it was during practice, in a meeting, or during a timeout in a game, players and coaches touched each other to show that everything they did would always be together.

TCU
W, 81–66

Tariq Owens throws down a dunk against TCU in Fort Worth on March 2, 2019. Owens recorded a double-double with 12 points and 13 rebounds as the Red Raiders improved to 12–4 in conference play with the road victory.

OVERTIME THRILLER TAKES STREAK TO SIX

OKLAHOMA STATE [W, 84–80]

THE RED RAIDERS extended their winning streak to six games with the victory over Oklahoma State, improved to 16–1 at home for the season, and tied Kansas State atop the conference standings. Tech committed only seven turnovers and owned a 44–34 rebounding advantage, but the Cowboys finished the game making 17 3-pointers including a last-second one by Lindy Waters to force overtime. Texas Tech, which finished the month of February with a 6–1 record, was 25-for-32 (78.1 percent) from the free-throw line, including going 5-for-6 in its first overtime session of the season.

Davide Moretti scored 20 points after going 12-for-12 at the free-throw line, Jarrett Culver recorded his third double-double of the season, and Tariq Owens provided 16 points and six rebounds in an 84–80 overtime win by the No. 11 Red Raiders. The game was tied at 71 after regulation on February 27, 2019, at the United Supermarkets Arena. But the Red Raiders dug deep and won in overtime.

"I think we have shown a lot of balance and we have different guys stepping up," Beard said.

"You're only as good as your last game, your last practice, your last rep, and we just have to continue being who we are," Beard said. "I've always thought you can learn from a victory just like you can from a defeat, and that's what we'll try to do in the next 24 hours."

TECH RIDES HIGH INTO SENIOR NIGHT

TEXAS (W, 70-51)

THE 18-ROUND FIGHT was going to come down to the wire as the Red Raiders took care of TCU, 81-66, and earned a 70-51 win over Texas on Senior Night at the United Supermarkets Arena. No. 18 Kansas State won on the road at TCU on March 4, 2019, keeping the Big 12 leaderboard knotted up.

The Red Raiders extended their winning streak to eight games, improved to 17-1 at home for the second straight season, and put themselves in position to win their first Big 12 title. Tech held an opponent under 55 points for the 12th time during the season and limited the Longhorns to only 29.6 percent shooting on the night.

"This is what it's all about," said Beard, who had improved to 50-5 at home in three seasons as Tech's head coach. "This is the thing we talk about. We always want to be a part of the fight. You want to be trying to play your best basketball during March."

Texas Tech honored its senior class of Norense Odiase, Brandone Francis, Tariq Owens, Matt Mooney, and Andrew Sorrells. Each senior scored and would combine for 36 points in the 19-point win to close out their careers on their home court.

"I'm just very fortunate and grateful," said Francis to reporters after the game. "As you can tell I don't even want to take my jersey off right now. I'll probably go to sleep with it on."

"We are playing our best ball, but I didn't know that we had an eight-game streak," Odiase said. "Honestly, I just have been taking it one day at a time. Especially with this game coming up. Everyone else looks at the bigger picture, but we look at each game and each opponent. That is how we got to this point."

Coach Beard with his seniors.

Brandone Francis puts up a layup in the win over Texas where he finished with 12 points on Senior Night.

Jarrett Culver scored a season-high 31 points and led Tech to an 80–73 win over Iowa State in the regular-season finale in Ames, Iowa. Culver was 12-for-19 from the field, including hitting four 3-pointers to secure the regular-season championship.

Matt Mooney puts up a shot against Iowa State in the regular-season finale. Mooney recorded 13 points, five assists, and four steals in the road win.

RED RAIDERS WIN BIG 12 TITLE IN AMES

IOWA STATE (W, 80-73)

TEXAS TECH WON this fight. For the first time in program history, the Red Raiders earned the Big 12 Conference regular-season championship.

The trophy came along after extending their streak to nine games with an 80-73 victory over Iowa State on March 9, 2019, at Hilton Coliseum in Ames, Iowa.

Texas Tech finished as co-champions with Kansas State, which secured a 68-53 win over Oklahoma on the same day in Manhattan, Kansas, to share the title. The Red Raiders, who also snapped a seven-game losing streak in Ames, had now won 13 regular-season titles in program history after winning six Southwest Conference regular-season titles (1961, 1962, 1973, 1985, 1995, 1996) and six Border Conference regular-season championships (1933, 1934, 1935, 1954, 1955, 1956).

"Our deal from the first day was to be a part of the fight," said Coach Beard in the postgame press conference. "The first year we were really competitive but we just couldn't win the close games. Last year we were right there down there down the stretch. To get here in our third year you have to give all of our players the credit. They are the ones that believed. You can imagine all the outside noises. It starts in recruiting when people say you can't win the Big 12 at Texas Tech. I've always disagreed. You get the right people in the locker room; it's all about culture and expectations."

Jarrett Culver scored a career-high 31 points, surpassing his previous career high of 30 points against Abilene Christian. He finished the game shooting 12-for-19 from the field and added four rebounds and three assists. He finished the regular season as the team leader, averaging 18.3 points, 6.2 rebounds, and 3.6 assists per game.

Brandone Francis drives to the basket in the win at Iowa State.

"I told him all week in preparation that we wouldn't need him to score 30," Beard said. "We needed him to have a great defensive game, share the ball, and take what the defense gave him. I was incorrect though. It's not the first time I was wrong in my life. We needed all those 31 he gave us. He's a special player and he'd be the first to tell you that he would give all his teammates who passed for him and screened for him all the credit. He's a really unselfish guy."

Culver is presented the Big 12 Player of the Year trophy by commissioner Bob Bowlsby prior to the start of the conference tournament in Kansas City.

It was all about celebrating team success for Texas Tech after the win at Iowa State, but the next morning turned to spotlighting some of the players who helped lead the Red Raiders to the program's first Big 12 Conference regular-season championship.

Texas Tech sophomore Jarrett Culver was named the Big 12 Conference Player of the Year. Culver, who was a unanimous All-Big 12 First-Team selection, was the first Red Raider to be named the Big 12 Player of the Year and led the team with 18.3 points, 6.2 rebounds, and 3.6 assists per game in his second season. Culver was only the fifth underclassman to earn the Big 12 Player of the Year honor, joining Marcus Smart (2012–13), Blake Griffin (2008–09), Michael Beasley (2007–08), and Kevin Durant (2006–07) for the league's top honor.

Culver finished the regular season by leading the Red Raiders with a career-high 31 points against the Cyclones and 982 total career points. Before leading Tech to the win at Iowa State he was named to the John R. Wooden National Ballot and was also a three-time Big 12 Conference Player of the Week during the season. Culver was one of the most consistently dominant players in the nation throughout the regular season, with nine games scoring over 20 points and having scored in double figures in 30 of 31 games. Culver, who was the 10th player in program history to earn Big 12 First-Team honors, averaged 17.6 points, 6.8 rebounds, 3.2 assists, and 1.4 steals per game in the 18 conference games this season.

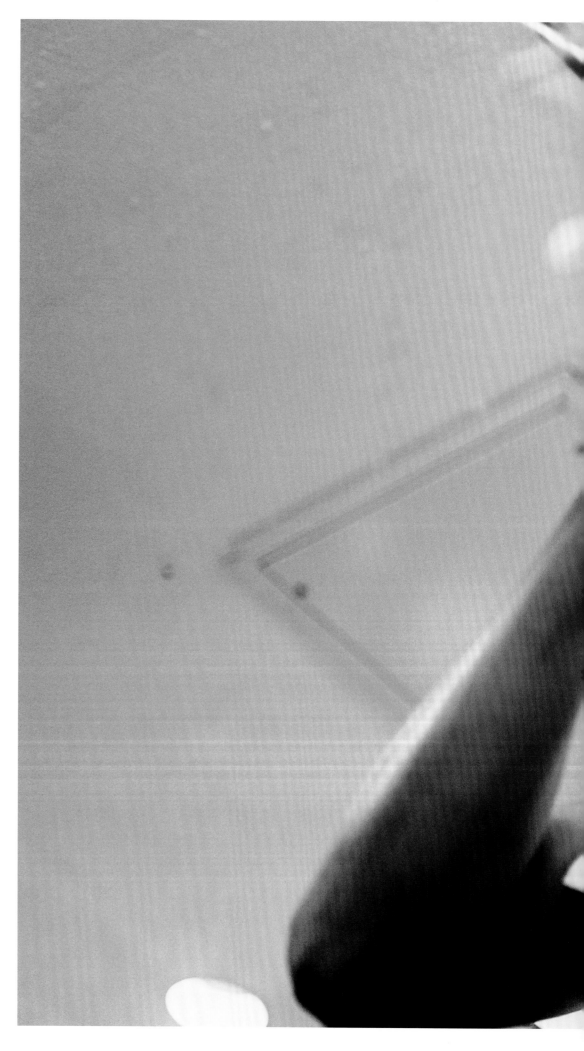

Head Coach Chris Beard rose to 101–34 as an NCAA Division I Coach, with a total record of 242–79. Beard, after the Red Raiders' win in Ames, had led the team to a 14–4 conference record and to the program's first Big 12 Conference title. The victory extended a nine-game winning streak to end the regular season and took Beard's record at Texas Tech to 71–29 over the past three years. He had been previously named the Big 12 Conference Co-Coach of the Year last season, and became-only the third coach in conference history to earn the award in back-to-back seasons, joining Bill Self and Larry Eustachy to receive two straight selections.

Mooney was tabbed for three honors with his All–Big 12 Second Team selection to go along with All–Big 12 Newcomer and All–Big 12 Defensive Team honors. A graduate transfer from Wauconda, Illinois, Mooney finished the regular season averaging 10.9 points, 3.3 assists, and 1.7 steals per game.

Beard and Texas Tech Director of Athletics Kirby Hocutt celebrate winning the conference title upon arriving back in Lubbock.

Texas Tech Chief of Staff Tim MacAllister celebrates the regular-season title with a kiss of the Big 12 Championship trophy.

Norense Odiase is surrounded by his teammates as he holds the championship trophy following the 80–73 road-win at Iowa State.

Davide Moretti earned All-Big 12 Third Team honors. Moretti led the nation by shooting 93.3 percent from the free-throw line and topped the conference by shooting 48.1 percent on 3-pointers. He was 25-for-39 (64.1 percent) on 3-pointers during the nine-game winning streak where he was also 33-for-34 on free throws and finished the regular season shooting 50.7 percent from the field.

Tariq Owens was an honorable mention selection. Owens produced one of the most dominant defensive seasons in Texas Tech history. He established a new program single-season record with 75 blocks going into the postseason, along with the single-game record with eight blocks against Memphis. Owens averaged 8.6 points, 5.7 rebounds, and 2.4 blocked shots per game going into the postseason.

Texas Tech led the nation by limiting teams to 36.8 percent shooting from the field. The team was second in the nation in opponent scoring, which was limited to only 58.6 points per game. With Owens at the lead, Tech averaged 4.9 blocks per game and led the Big 12 with a plus-3.3 turnover margin.

WINNING STREAK ENDS AS RAIDERS PREPARE FOR THE TOURNAMENT

WEST VIRGINIA [L, 74-79]

LOSING TO WEST VIRGINIA in the Big 12 Championship quarterfinals was in no way part of the plan, but the Red Raiders returned to Lubbock on Friday morning and got back to work. The Selection Show was two days away and the team's story was just getting started. One can look back now and say it was a good thing that the team got some rest and time to refocus before the NCAA tournament, but no one was thinking that in Kansas City that night. Beard's team wanted to win every game, and they took this sting with them into the next chapter.

It was to be the most important one yet.

BOB WISCHUSEN (ESPN): "From the first Chris Beard practice our crew was at last season, you could see the foundation being built, the buy-in from his players. It was fun to watch the story of a program develop first hand, and shock so many who hadn't seen them play until the NCAA Tournament. A team that worked as hard as the Red Raiders did deserve to have a special season."

GEOFF HAXTON (TTSN): "From the head coach down to the managers, no team outworked the Red Raiders. Unselfish and talented players combined with unmatched work ethic made Texas Tech a force every time they took the court."

JIM NANTZ (CBS): "They are extremely well prepared, smart, and intense with their approach to every aspect of the game. From the eye test, as I prepare for the game by watching Texas Tech, this is a great basketball team capable of winning the championship."

BILL RAFTERY (CBS): "I've watched them now at three practices and the Kansas game, which I bring up just to show their resiliency. They have a toughness about them that they've shown at multiple times throughout the season. You talk to coaches throughout the country and they don't want to play against Beard and his team because they shut you down and are efficient offensively. His players give him everything and it shows by the way they play together."

GRANT HILL (CBS): "There is a spirit about this team that comes across on TV and watching them on tape where you can tell they enjoy playing together and for one another. The way they compete is fun to watch. Watching them practice the last two days I understand more why. They have energy, connectivity, communication, and great leadership from their coach and players. It's a special group. Every group has a unique style and personality and Tech has created a real fun atmosphere to play for and for us to watch."

PART IV:
THE DANCE

From the Coach Beard Glossary:

Smell the Roses – We wanted to be one of the teams that put ourselves in a position to win the whole thing and part of that was a plan. It started for us with smelling the roses. We wanted to embrace the NCAA Tournament and the fact that we had won the Big 12 regular-season championship. We weren't going to shy away from enjoying the experience. We were going to enjoy every bus ride, flight, meal, press conference, practice, and game.

Be Us – When it came time to play the game, we wanted to be the same team that had won the Big 12, that had earned a three seed. We didn't want to change who we were just because of the stage we were now on. I thought our guys did a great job of being themselves throughout everything all season.

SELECTION SUNDAY

GATHERED TOGETHER for the NCAA Selection Sunday, Texas Tech heard its named called as the No. 3 seed in the West Region, where the Red Raiders would match up to play Northern Kentucky in the opening round in Tulsa.

"We worked hard for this," said Coach Beard at a press conference following the announcement. "This is something we've been talking about since the spring in our recruiting, summer workouts, and in the fall preseason work. Through the ups and downs, we continued talking about getting into this tournament. You never take it for granted. I want to make sure these guys enjoy the ride, not just the destination."

"Coach talks about soaking it in," Mooney said. "During the selection show, instead of being on my phone I wanted to enjoy it. It was a really cool experience and is something you should enjoy. Then there's a point where you have to lock in and go win. We have to go get ready for Northern Kentucky now and get our mind set on that."

Tariq Owens looks for options in the first round of the NCAA Tournament win over Northern Kentucky. Owens finished the game with 12 points to help lead the Red Raiders to the 72-57 win over the Norse.

ONE WIN IN: TECH DOWNS NKU IN NCAA FIRST ROUND

NORTHERN KENTUCKY UNIVERSITY [W, 72-57]

Chris Beard celebrates a big play for the Red Raiders who opened their NCAA Tournament run with an impressive win over Northern Kentucky in Tulsa, Oklahoma.

JARRETT CULVER went for 29 points, eight rebounds, and seven assists; Tariq Owens added five blocks; and Matt Mooney recorded eight assists to help lead No. 3 seed Texas Tech to a 72-57 first-round win over No. 14 Northern Kentucky on March 22, 2019, at the BOK Center in Tulsa.

"We're trying to win two games in three days," said Coach Beard after the win. "The first game of the tournament is always the toughest. Just really proud of our guys tonight and our team effort. I thought we won this game as a team. I think in the second half, more than any big adjustment, we just wanted to stay aggressive."

Up only four at halftime, Texas Tech would take its first double-digit lead of the game at 44-34 on an Owens layup with 15 minutes to play. The advantage would dip to single digits for a brief moment a minute later before an alley-oop from Mooney to Owens sparked a 6-0 run that had the Red Raiders up 15 with 11 to play. Tech would control the rest of the game and led by as much as 20 on a Moretti layup that pushed it to 70-50.

"We thought in the first half we played well offensively, we couldn't make a free throw, and we had too many turnovers," Beard said. "Really kind of staying consistent with our original game plan with just an emphasis of getting a little bit more aggressive."

Culver established a new program record by scoring 29 points in an NCAA game, passing Ronald Ross who had 28 against UCLA in the 2005 tournament. The Big 12 Conference Player of the Year was 10-for-17 from the field with three 3-pointers and six free throws to go along with having five steals for the second straight game and the fourth time this season.

"We just focused on us, details, how we got so far and how we made a run in the Big 12 and how we got to the March Madness tournament," Culver said. "So I felt like we focused on this all weekend. We did a great job on that."

Owens established a new program high in an NCAA game with his five blocked shots and now has 83 for the season. A graduate transfer playing in his first NCAA Tournament game, Owens was 6-for-7 from the field and had three rebounds.

64   32   16   8   4   2

Norense Odiase puts up a shot in the win over Northern Kentucky.

Brandone Francis focuses on defense against NKU, helping the Red Raiders limit the Norse to 37.1 percent shooting in the game.

TTU (3) vs. NKU (14)
Final Score: 72-57
March 22, 2019 • Tulsa, Oklahoma

	FG	3-PT	Reb	Ast	Pts
Norense Odiase	2-3	0-0	3	0	4
Tariq Owens	6-7	0-1	3	0	12
Matt Mooney	3-8	1-2	3	8	9
Jarrett Culver	10-17	3-5	8	7	29
Davide Moretti	4-10	0-4	5	2	10
Brandone Francis	2-3	2-3	3	1	6
Deshawn Corprew	1-3	0-1	3	0	2
Kyler Edwards	0-2	0-1	1	0	0

Tariq Owens grabs a loose ball and kicks it out to Davide Moretti to maintain possession for the Red Raiders.

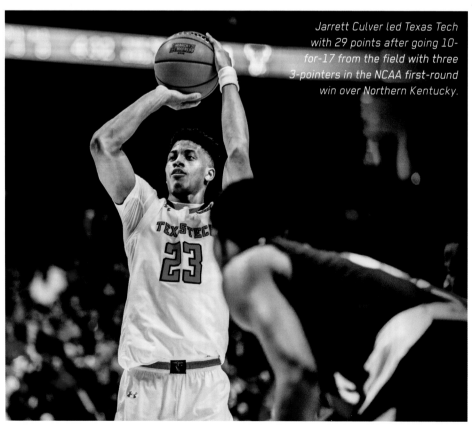

Jarrett Culver led Texas Tech with 29 points after going 10-for-17 from the field with three 3-pointers in the NCAA first-round win over Northern Kentucky.

Matt Mooney drives to the basket in the win over Northern Kentucky

Davide Moretti goes up for a layup in the win over Northern Kentucky. Moretti finished the game with 10 points for the Red Raiders, who shot 52.8 percent from the field.

Texas Tech senior Norense Odiase and freshman Kyler Edwards celebrate the win over Northern Kentucky.

MARCHING ON: TECH ADVANCES WITH 20-POINT WIN OVER BUFFALO

UNIVERSITY OF BUFFALO (W, 78-58)

TEXAS TECH earned its way to the Sweet 16 for the second straight season after locking down a 78-58 win over No. 6 Buffalo. Norense Odiase and Jarrett Culver both recorded double-doubles, and the defense held the Bulls to 30 points below their season scoring average at the BOK Center in Tulsa.

"We're not supposed to be here," Coach Beard said. "These guys have continued to keep a chip on their shoulder and just realize that we can do a lot of things if we play as a team. I thought that's what we did tonight, we guarded at a high level. Had different guys step up offensively until the game got all sloppy late, but one of our cleaner games this year. For Texas Tech basketball, the story this year is team. Play for the guy next to us. I've never been more proud of a team I coached."

The program returned to the NCAA Sweet 16 round for the fourth time in program history (1996, 2005, 2018, 2019).

"The NCAA Tournament is like Disney World to us," Beard said. "They're involved in basketball. It's all we think about. It's what makes Norense get up at 5:30 in the morning in the summers. It's what makes Culver come in at 10 p.m., seven nights a week, to get shots up. It's what ultimately makes us coaches do what we do. This is it."

Texas Tech led by as many as 29 in the game and outscored the Bulls 45-33 in the second half, including a 7-1 run to start the half that pushed the lead to 40-26 and then a 10-0 run for a commanding 51-30 lead with 12 minutes to play. Buffalo's season ended with a 32-4 overall record. Their loss to the Red Raiders snapped a 13-game winning streak. Tech made only five 3-pointers in the game but dominated inside with a 30-18 scoring advantage in the paint and also had an 18-9 advantage on points after turnovers. Buffalo's first and only lead of the night was at 25-24 with 3:24 remaining in the first half before the Red Raiders scored the final nine points of the half and continued the momentum throughout the rest of the game.

Odiase established a new Texas Tech tournament record by securing 15 rebounds and added a season-high 14 points. The 15 rebounds were a career high and the sixth time this season he recorded 10 or more rebounds. Culver produced his fifth double-double of the season by leading the Red Raiders with 16 points and having 10 rebounds. Culver led Tech with 29 points in their first-round win over Northern Kentucky and added five assists and two steals in the win over the Bulls. Kyler Edwards had six points with a team-leading two 3-pointers. Brandone Francis and Deshawn Corprew added five points each off the bench for the Red Raiders. Moretti finished the game 5-for-6 at the free-throw line and added two assists. Odiase's 15 rebounds set a new program record, passing Tony Battie (1996), Mike Russell (1976), and Rick Bullock (1976) who each had 14-rebound performances in NCAA Tournament games.

"That's the process that every day the grind is thinking about that game, trying to get back to that level with a new team, a new team

64   **32**   16   8   4   2

Tariq Owens puts up a shot in the 20-point win over Buffalo in the NCAA Tournament second round. Owens finished the game with 10 points and seven rebounds to help lead the Red Raiders to the Sweet 16.

that nobody thought they could get to that level," Odiase said. "We're proving it so far. We've got to keep going. The process got us here and the process will take us as far as we need to go. That's all it's been."

Tech's defense held the Bulls to 0-for-9 shooting to start the second half before they would make their first shot eight minutes into the half. By that time, the Red Raiders owned a 53-30 lead in a game that was close in the first half but never resembled that again in the second half. The Bulls were limited to 36.5 percent shooting in the game after coming into the night shooting 46.4 percent from the field and averaging 85.1 points per game.

Tariq Owens had 10 points and seven rebounds for the Red Raiders in the game. He and Odiase both went 4-for-4 from the field, while Matt Mooney and Davide Moretti added 11 each. The Red Raiders shot 48.2 percent from the field and were 19-for-25 from the free-throw line in the win.

At halftime, Texas Tech had limited Buffalo to 36 percent shooting and to only 3-for-10 from beyond the arc. The Red Raiders were shooting 41.4 percent and were 7-for-9 at the free-throw line, but also struggled by going 2-for-9 on 3-pointers. Tech had six assists on 12 baskets in the opening half.

Jarrett Culver led Texas Tech by going for a double-double with 16 points and 10 rebounds in the win over Buffalo on March 24, 2019 in Tulsa, Oklahoma.

Davide Moretti recorded 11 points in the win over Buffalo.

TTU (3) vs. Buffalo (6)
Final Score: 78–58
March 24, 2019 • Tulsa, Oklahoma

	FG	3-PT	Reb	Ast	Pts
Norense Odiase	4-4	0-0	15	1	14
Tariq Owens	4-4	0-0	7	1	10
Matt Mooney	4-15	1-4	4	1	11
Jarrett Culver	6-17	1-4	10	5	16
Davide Moretti	3-7	0-3	4	2	11
Brandone Francis	2-5	0-2	3	0	5
Deshawn Corprew	2-2	1-1	3	0	5
Kyler Edwards	2-2	2-2	0	1	6
Avery Benson	0-1	0-0	0	0	0

Texas Tech senior Norense Odiase recorded a double-double with 15 rebounds and 14 points in 78–58 win over Buffalo in the NCAA second round. Odiase was 4-for-4 from the field and 6-for-7 from the line in the game where he had a career high with the 15 rebounds.

Matt Mooney puts up a layup for two of his 11 points against Buffalo.

SWEET UPSET: TECH DOMINATES MICHIGAN

UNIVERSITY OF MICHIGAN [W, 63-44]

IT WAS AN UPSET on paper, but not to Texas Tech.

Playing with the confidence and poise they had all season, the Red Raiders dismantled the No. 2-seeded Wolverines on their way to the Elite Eight. Culver went off for 22 points, Davide Moretti added 15 more, and Tariq Owens had 10 rebounds.

"I'm just really pleased and happy for our players to advance," Coach Beard said. "We came to Anaheim to play 80 minutes, so we're halfway there. But the top of our list of why I'm so happy for our guys is I think we just beat one of the best teams we've played all year. We guarded at a high level, played team basketball, and played eight guys in the rotation."

Tech stifled Michigan, who had only 16 points at halftime. The Red Raiders poured it on with a 12-2 run to start the second half. The Wolverines were limited to 32.7 percent shooting in the game—including going 1-for-19 on 3-pointers, good for an abysmal 5.3 percent. The Red Raiders committed only eight turnovers in the win and forced 14, the exact mark Beard had preached to his team would send them to the next round.

Culver went 9-for-19 from the field and added four assists. Moretti, who had not made a 3 in the past two games, led the Red Raiders with three in the game on four attempts.

"I feel like we stayed true to ourselves," Culver said. "We played the defense we've been playing all year and their shots wasn't going in. We had urgency."

Texas Tech was held to 35.7 percent shooting in the first half but would explode in the second half by shooting 51.9 percent from the field and 7-for-8 at the free-throw line. The Red Raiders finished the game with 12 assists as a team, including four each from Moretti and Culver.

"I thought we shared the ball more," Beard said. "Half of our baskets tonight were assisted. That's always the objective. I thought we trusted each other, the ball got moving better the second half, and the shooting is always going to be the law: you put in the time, shots are going to go down. We were fortunate tonight. Michigan didn't shoot the ball well. But you have to give our guys credit. I love the way we were sharing the ball, getting assists, and we had nice balance. Several guys stepped up and made shots."

Tech finished the game with six 3-pointers with freshman Kyler Edwards making one, while senior Norense Odiase contributed four rebounds and Brandone Francis added four points.

"They have a really good team and they have some really good shooters," said Owens of Michigan. "For our game plan, we knew we had to have a lot of urgency in getting out there because they're a really good team."

The Red Raiders took their first double-digit lead of the game at 26-16 coming out of halftime with Mooney hitting a jumper in the lane and pushed it to 13 with Moretti hitting his second 3-pointer of the game on the next possession. A huge alley-oop dunk by

64   32   16   8   4   2

Owens on a pass from Moretti was followed by a 3-pointer by Moretti, giving the Red Raiders a 34–18 lead with 17 minutes to play. The score was doubled up at 36–18 when Owens threw down a one-handed dunk off an assist to give the Red Raiders a 7–0 run that had pushed an eight-point lead to 18 in the first four minutes of the half.

The Red Raiders never looked back.

Culver would assert his dominance midway through the second half by going on a 9–2 run of his own that gave the Red Raiders a 50–29 lead with 9:41 remaining before Francis hit a layup that pushed the lead to 23 a minute later. After a Michigan basket, Mooney drilled a 3-pointer to give the Red Raiders a 25-point lead with eight on the clock.

"I've always thought that was the key is in March everybody has to play well," Beard said. "Sounds like Captain Obvious, but you have to bring something to the game and I thought the eight guys we played tonight really did and we were locked in on defense and we had just enough assists to keep our offense balance. I thought the guys played well. I'm pleased I get to coach these guys another day, another pregame meal, another practice tomorrow. I don't want this to end, man. These guys are so fun to coach."

TTU (3) vs. Michigan (2)
Final Score: 63-44
March 28, 2019 • Anaheim, California

	FG	3-PT	Reb	Ast	Pts
Norense Odiase	0-1	0-0	4	0	0
Tariq Owens	2-7	0-1	10	0	7
Matt Mooney	4-9	2-4	3	2	10
Jarrett Culver	9-19	0-5	4	4	22
Davide Moretti	5-7	3-4	1	4	15
Brandone Francis	2-7	0-3	0	2	4
Deshawn Corprew	1-4	0-1	4	0	2
Kyler Edwards	1-1	1-1	1	0	3

Tariq Owens played lock-down defense against Michigan, finishing with two blocks and 10 rebounds in the win that sent the Red Raiders to their second straight NCAA Elite Eight.

Jarrett Culver approaches Tariq Owens on the court after a big play by Owens against Michigan in the Sweet 16. The Red Raiders won 63–44 over the Wolverines to advance to the Elite Eight where they would match up against Gonzaga in Anaheim, California.

Brandone Francis and the Red Raiders limited the Wolverines to 16 points in the first half and to 32.7 percent shooting in the game. Michigan was held to 1-for-19 from beyond the arc by the tenacious defense.

Street Dogs in California. After rolling through the first two rounds of the NCAA tournament in Oklahoma, the Red Raiders were in the Sweet 16 for the second straight season and found themselves in Anaheim, California. Only 16 teams remained and Tech was there by being themselves. After the first practice in California, Tech's assistant coaches and managers sprinted onto the court barking in a continuation of a theme that epitomized the underdog mentality that the Red Raiders embraced.

ELITE EIGHT WIN: TECH OUTLASTS GONZAGA

GONZAGA UNIVERSITY (W, 75-69)

TEXAS TECH ADVANCED to the Final Four for the first time in program history after earning a 75-69 win over Gonzaga for the NCAA West Region Championship. Jarrett Culver recorded 19 points and six rebounds, and Davide Moretti hit a pair of crucial 3-pointers down the stretch at the Honda Center in Anaheim, California.

"Texas Tech is going to the Final Four," said Coach Chris Beard at the postgame press conference. "Some of you look surprised."

The No. 3-seeded Red Raiders reached the Elite Eight for the first time the prior season and returned with the goal of creating more history after also winning their first Big 12 Conference regular-season championship. Tech did that by holding the top-seeded Bulldogs to under 70 points for only the fourth time in their season.

"How about our four seniors," Beard said. "The backbone of our team. Norense and Brandone, a big part of our success. Tariq and Matt as grad transfers buying into our culture so quickly. It's like they've been here for their whole careers. I've always loved our seniors but never been more proud of the four guys to my left right now. They're really the story of Tech basketball this year. I'm glad I get to coach them again. The Final Four is awesome and all that, but the most cool thing is I get to coach these guys again. We get to get after it again in practice and travel and spend time together. That's going to be a special week for us."

Texas Tech knocked off Gonzaga by shooting 44 percent from the field, hitting nine 3-pointers, and making 16-for-19 at the

free-throw line. On defense, the Red Raiders limited Gonzaga to 42 percent shooting and forced 16 turnovers in what was perceived as an upset.

Culver led the team with 19 points and was named the West Region's Most Outstanding Player, while Matt Mooney added 17 points and Moretti went for 12 with his two 3-pointers that helped push the Red Raiders to the win over the Bulldogs. Tariq Owens finished the game with nine points, seven rebounds, and three blocked shots, Brandone Francis added six points, and freshman Kyler Edwards went for eight points.

64   32   16   8   4   2

"It's huge, for our program, for our city, for us personally, for our family, our friends, it's huge," Odiase said. "Everything we worked for starting off in the summer—the workouts, the retreat, the battles we've been through, the struggles, man. It's huge. It means the world to work so hard and it pay off. It definitely hasn't hit me. Hasn't hit us, I don't think, yet. But it's huge for all of us and we're just so excited that we get to play with each other again."

Mooney and Culver were both named to the all-tournament team for the Red Raiders, joined by Gonzaga's Brandon Clarke and Rui Hachimura and Florida State's Trent Forrest. Culver scored 12 of his 19 points in the second half and is now averaging 21.5 points per game through four NCAA Tournament contests. Mooney led the Red Raiders with 11 points in the first half, finished the game shooting 6-for-12 from the field, and hit 4-for-4 at the free-throw line. Culver made seven free throws in the game and Moretti was 2-for-2 at the line, which took him to 95 of 103 (92.2 percent) for the season.

Texas Tech took a 66–60 lead after a pair of Moretti 3-pointers with 1:46 on the clock. The lead grew to 69–62 following a pair of free throws by Culver and then one by Francis. Down seven with 44 seconds remaining, the Bulldogs cut into the lead with a layup by Josh Perkins, who then hit a 3-pointer after a Red Raider turnover with 22 seconds remaining to make it a two-point game.

Tech would finish off the game by going 6-for-6 at the free-throw line. Mooney, Moretti, and Culver made two each.

"Growing up my whole life watching these press conferences, games, and all that, and the guy that always gets there and says indescribable, and I'm like, oh, give us something better than that," said Beard of his thoughts when cutting down the net. "But I don't have anything better. It's indescribable. I think a lot about those four seniors, great leadership on this year's team, and I think about all the guys that came before us, seeing Coach Gerald Myers as happy as he is, a great Texas Tech coach and great AD, and I think about everybody else but myself in those moments."

Kyler Edwards puts up a shot in the NCAA Elite Eight win over Gonzaga where he went for eight points. Edwards hit two 3-pointers in the game for the Red Raiders who hit nine shots from beyond the arc against the Bulldogs.

Jarrett Culver drives in for two of his team-leading 19 points in the win over Gonzaga. Culver, who hit two 3-pointers, was 7-for-8 from the free-throw line to help the Red Raiders advance to the program's first-ever NCAA Final Four.

Davide Moretti helps Tariq Owens up from the court after a hustle play. The Red Raiders forced 16 turnovers and had seven blocked shots in the game, three coming from Owens.

TTU (3) vs. Gonzaga (1)
Final Score: 75-69
March 30, 2019 • Anaheim, California

	FG	3-PT	Reb	Ast	Pts
Norense Odiase	2-2	0-0	1	0	4
Tariq Owens	4-5	1-1	7	0	9
Matt Mooney	6-12	1-4	2	5	17
Jarrett Culver	5-19	2-8	5	2	19
Davide Moretti	4-9	2-4	2	2	12
Brandone Francis	2-6	1-3	2	1	6
Deshawn Corprew	0-0	0-0	1	1	0
Kyler Edwards	2-4	2-3	3	0	8

Davide Moretti directs a play during the win over Michigan where he went for 12 points with two 3-pointers. Moretti, who had been surprised two nights earlier by the arrival of his parents and brother from Italy, shined in California to help the Red Raiders advance to the Final Four.

Moretti said: "It was amazing for me. My mom had never watched me play here, so it was kind of special for me and I play for my team first of all and then for my family right after that. It was really a special moment for me."

Chris Beard celebrates Tech's NCAA West Region Championship with his daughters, Avery, Ella, and Margo following the win over Gonzaga on March 30, 2019 in Anaheim, California.

Texas Tech staff
Max Lefevre, Tim
MacAllister, and Matt
Temple celebrate the
win over Gonzaga on
the court together.

Coach Beard cuts the final piece of the net in celebration of the West Region title.

Davide Moretti exits the court following Tech's win over Michigan State at the Final Four.

WHY NOT US?: TECH STORMS PAST SPARTANS

MICHIGAN STATE UNIVERSITY [W, 61-51]

CHRIS BEARD told his Red Raiders that it was going to happen, and they believed him. Only four teams in the nation were still playing on April 6, 2019, and as the night came to an end only two remained.

"He told us in the summer. I don't know if it was the first day, but it was early," Matt Mooney said. "He said, we have enough in this gym, in this locker room right here to play on the final Monday night, and either Coach is psychic, or, well, he might just be psychic."

Texas Tech advanced to the national championship final after closing out a 61-51 semifinal win over Michigan State on a 9-0 run and limiting the Spartans to 31.9 percent shooting in front of 72,711 fans in attendance at U.S. Bank Stadium in Minneapolis, Minnesota. From being unranked starting the season to eliminating the Spartans to set up a final against Virginia, the Red Raiders were now one victory away from winning a national title.

"I'm just really happy for these guys," Beard said. "We knew we weren't going to out-tough Michigan State, but we wanted to try to match their toughness. In the basketball game, there were some things we had to get done. We knew it had to be a low turnover game. I think we had one or two turnovers in the second half, so that gave us a chance. We had some big-time individual performances when we needed them most. We're excited to live another day and get to play on Monday night."

The Red Raiders, who were making their first Final Four appearance in program history and broke the school record with their 31st win of the season, improved to 8-1 in the NCAA Tournament under Coach Beard after holding an opponent to under 60 points for the 19th time. Tech had only seven turnovers and limited the Spartans (32-7) to only 7-for-24 (29.2 percent) on 3-pointers.

Matt Mooney led the Red Raiders with 22 points, while Jarrett Culver added 10 points and five rebounds. Norense Odiase pulled down nine rebounds, and Tariq Owens had three blocks and seven points. Brandone Francis contributed nine points and Kyler Edwards six from the bench, while Davide Moretti had five to help lead the Red Raiders to their first national final appearance in program history.

"They're great players, great interior players," Odiase said of the Spartans. "They're tough, gritty. We just tried to do a good job on them, slow them down as best as we can. Not just me and Tariq, but our whole team since we switched. I thought our smaller guys battled. They really fought and they were able to help us keep switching the whole game, and it just helped us towards our game plan."

Tech led 23-21 at halftime and would never trail in the second half but did see the Spartans cut the lead to one at 52-51 with 2:54 to play. With the gap down to one, Culver hit a jumper and then a free throw to make it a four-point lead and then popped a 3-pointer for a 58-51 lead. Two free throws by Odiase and another by Culver sealed the double-digit win.

64   32   16   8   4   2

"On behalf of everybody in our program, I just want to con-gratulate Michigan State on another Final Four berth, cham-pionship season," Beard said. "I have so much respect for them. When you're in games like this and you have a week to prepare, I basically watched every game Michigan State played this year, every interview, every article, and you kind of get to know somebody. This is one of the class programs of all of college basketball. Coach [Tom] Izzo's handshake and kind words to me after the game is something I'll never forget in my career. So personally, that was pretty cool."

Mooney matched a season high with 22 points to lead the Red Raiders after hitting four 3-pointers and going 8-for-16 from the field. Mooney scored 13 of his 22 points in the second half where he was 3-for-5 from beyond the arc.

"He's obviously very, very talented, but the thing that really impressed me tonight was just his courage, just to be able to make those big plays and want to be in those moments," Beard said. "When Culver was — I'm not going to say strug-gling a little bit — I think when Michigan State was focused on Culver so much, Matt had the courage to step up and take those shots. He's making plays on both ends. I loved his poise tonight. He's a special player."

The Red Raiders finished the game with nine 3-pointers and shot 43.1 percent from the field in the game, including going 14-for-25 (56.0 percent) in the second half. Tech was 5-for-10 from beyond the arc in the second half and committed only two turnovers in the final 20 minutes of the game. Culver scored nine of his 10 points in the second half and had two assists in the game.

Asked in the postgame press conference about the unlikelihood of a team going from unranked to start the season to playing in the national championship game, Beard exposed the chip on his shoulder and explained the team's mentality.

"I respect the question, but why not us?" he asked. "We've got good players. We've got a great university. We play in arguably the best league in the country. We won the Big 12 regular-season title. We're a good team. We've got good players. Yeah, I think we deserve to be here, as do a lot of other teams. You've got to get fortunate, but we did believe. I'm looking forward to coaching these guys on Monday night."

Texas Tech uniforms hang in the lockers at the Final Four in Minneapolis, Minnesota.

TTU (3) vs. MSU (2)
Final Score: 61–51

April 6, 2019 • Minneapolis, Minnesota

	FG	3-PT	Reb	Ast	Pts
Norense Odiase	0-0	0-0	9	2	2
Tariq Owens	3-4	1-2	4	0	7
Matt Mooney	8-16	4-8	3	1	22
Jarrett Culver	3-12	1-3	5	2	10
Davide Moretti	2-6	1-4	2	0	5
Brandone Francis	4-8	1-4	2	2	9
Deshawn Corprew	0-0	0-0	1	0	0
Kyler Edwards	2-5	1-2	4	1	6

The Red Raiders hold each other back before running onto the court of their open practice at the Final Four.

Beard, with the help of his daughter, Ella, reminds the Red Raiders to "smell the roses" during the Final Four open-practice session.

The Red Raiders go through a closed-practice workout at U.S. Bank Stadium in Minneapolis, Minnesota.

Texas Tech prior to the start of the open-practice session at the Final Four.

Matt Mooney drives to the basket against Michigan State at the Final Four. Mooney matched a season high by going for 22 points against the Spartans where he was 8-for-16 from the field with four 3-pointers for the Red Raiders.

The Red Raider starters huddle together at center court before the start of their Final Four semifinal matchup against Michigan State.

Davide Moretti hustles for a loose ball against Michigan State's All-America guard Cassius Winston in Texas Tech's 61–51 win over the Spartans in the Final Four. The Red Raiders forced 11 turnovers in the game and limited their turnovers to only seven to advance to the NCAA National Championship Final.

Texas Tech uniforms hang in the lockers at the Final Four in Minneapolis, Minnesota.

Chris Beard celebrates as he leaves the court following the win over Michigan State in the Final Four.

Matt Mooney advances Texas Tech on the bracket in the locker room after he went off for 22 points in the win over Michigan State at the Final Four.

The Final Four patch was on a Texas Tech uniform for the first time in history and a lifetime of memories were made by the achievement. Playing at the highest level of college basketball, the Red Raiders were joined by Michigan State, Auburn, and Virginia in Minneapolis, Minnesota for the Final Four. It was a week of amazing experiences, from practicing in front of more than 20,000 fans to filming promotional videos for the CBS telecast.

Coach Beard and Texas Tech University President Lawrence Schovanec celebrate the win over Michigan State in the locker room after the victory.

Thousands of fans greeted the team upon its arrival at 2:30 a.m. at the United Supermarkets Arena following the win over Gonzaga that sent the program to its first Final Four appearance.

TARIQ OWENS WILLS HIS WAY TO THE CHAMPIONSHIP GAME

WHILE THE TEAM was jubilant at having made the final, the celebration was immediately tempered with doubt that one of Tech's most important players would make the last lineup of the year.

However, there was never a doubt for Tariq Owens that he was going to play on Monday night. He believed it when Chris Beard convinced him to spend his last season in Lubbock. He believed it when the coach told the team it was possible in the summer and during the team retreat, when they were picked seventh in the Big 12 preseason poll and unranked nationally. It was a belief he had all season, and even a severe ankle injury in the Final Four semifinal wasn't going to prevent him from being there for his team.

"I just have that by-any-means mentality," Owens said. "It was my final year in college, first time ever being in the tournament, and playing in the Final Four has always been a dream so I wasn't going to let anything stop me from playing."

At 14:43 in the second half of the win over Michigan State, Owens went up and blocked All-American Cassius Winston's shot in the lane. It was his 91st block of the season and came with the Red Raiders leading by three. Previously in the game he had taken

another hard fall to the court after a rebound and diving for a loose ball into the scorer's table. Owens was giving the Red Raiders everything he had, just as he had all season.

The 91st block came at a price though, with Owens's right foot awkwardly landing on Norense Odiase's foot. It was one of those wincing moments, when a stadium of more than 72,000 goes silent and all players, on both teams, instantaneously transition from fierce competition to extreme concern. Owens lay there on the court, rolling in pain, screaming in agony and biting his hand.

"When Tariq went down in the Final Four, my initial fear was a broken leg," said Texas Tech Athletic Trainer Chris Williams. "After evaluating him on the floor and ruling out any obvious fracture we took him back to the locker room for further evaluation. His ankle swelled immediately, but Tariq's attitude was always positive. He told me, 'I've sprained my ankle before. I've waited my whole life for this moment. Tape it tight, I'm going back in.' The doctor and I cleared him and he went back in, running out to the court in dramatic fashion."

At 6:52 on the clock, the crowd erupted as Owens and Williams came jogging out of the tunnel to the court. The ankle was swollen, but the dedicated player wasn't going to miss being out there as the Red Raiders finished off the biggest win in program history.

After the game, the ankle continued to swell, and as adrenaline dissipated, the pain became unbearable. Owens danced with his teammates some but not to the extent that he normally had. During the media's open locker room session, Owens, Williams, and doctors had already slipped back to the training room to get to work. His mind was on Monday night and he knew that it wouldn't be easy.

"After the game he came to me and he told me he trusted that I'll get him well enough to play Monday," Williams said. "I told him that

I'll stay up all night the next two nights if you're committed. We made a deal; we worked around the clock for literally 48 hours and he gave it his best. His fight was unlike anything I've ever seen. He never for a second doubted that he'd be ready to play."

"He had a severe high-ankle sprain, these ones where some guys are out for two or three weeks," said Beard about Owens after the national championship game. "In the normal bas-ketball season, he would not have played tonight. Tariq is a no-excuse guy. You're not going to hear this from his camp, but I'll proudly tell anyone that wants to know, the guy is a war-rior. I think it was just adrenaline that let him get back in the game the other night, and then after the game it swelled up. Our trainer, Chris Williams, did a great job, worked tirelessly around the clock. I have nothing but respect for Tariq. Most guys wouldn't even try. He's just a warrior."

The final game on Monday night was one befitting this warrior mentality.

TIME RUNS OUT FOR A NATIONAL CHAMPIONSHIP

UNIVERSITY OF VIRGINIA [L, 77-85]

THE RED RAIDERS' historic run to a championship fell short in heartbreaking fashion. They finished as the 2019 NCAA Runner-Up despite overcoming a 10-point deficit in the second half to force overtime before the University of Virginia (UVA) won the national championship with an 85-77 victory on that final Monday night in Minnesota.

"The game was everything we thought it would be," Beard said. "I thought it would come down to one last possession, and it did in regulation, and then in overtime it just got away from us a little bit. Nothing but respect for their program, their coaches, their players, their fans. I thought it was a great National Championship Game. In terms of our players, I've never been more proud of a team that I've coached. There's a lot of emotion in our locker room right now, and it's real, just guys that care about the guy next to them."

Virginia connected on a game-tying 3-pointer with 12 seconds remaining in regulation and then used an 11-0 run in overtime to win its first national title. It was the first championship final to go to overtime since 2008 and the eighth ever. The Red Raiders (31-7) completed their season as the winningest team in program history, the first to win the Big 12 Conference regular season and the first to advance to the Final Four and national final. Those accomplishments will all be something to cherish, but on Monday night, as Virginia celebrated, the Red Raiders were forced to live the reality of sports.

"Resilience and toughness, everything we are as a team," said Odiase in the postgame press conference. "It took a lot to get here. We've been through a lot together. Total new team one year, and to get here, it took a lot of guts. I'm proud of our team for that, but it doesn't feel good at all right now."

Down 53-43 with 10:24 remaining in regulation, Tech started chipping away. They got it to 59-56 on a Matt Mooney 3-pointer and tied the game with Odiase converting an and-one a minute later. After the Cavaliers pushed their lead back to four, Davide Moretti stepped up and hit a huge 3-pointer to cut it to one, and Jarrett Culver gave the Red Raiders their first lead at 66-65 with 35 seconds to play. Tech went up three on a pair of free throws by Odiase

64   32   16   8   4   2

before UVA's De'Andre Hunter forced overtime with a corner 3-pointer with 14 seconds remaining.

In overtime, a Mooney 3-pointer and jumper gave the Red Raiders a 73-70 lead before the Cavaliers went on an 11-0 run to take control and secure their program's first national championship. Tech was limited to 4-for-11 shooting in overtime, including going 1-for-5 on 3-pointers. The Raiders were outscored 17-9 in the final five minutes of the game, when the Cavaliers went 12-for-12 on free throws in overtime and had a 7-3 rebounding advantage.

"We felt like we had momentum because we came back from about 10," Culver said. "We for sure felt like we had momentum. Our mindset was just a five-minute game; we've been prepared for it, we practice it every day. We just didn't come out on top tonight."

Tech finished the game shooting 42.9 percent from the field with 10 3-pointers and limited itself to eight turnovers, but the Cavaliers were able to shoot 45.8 percent from the field against the Red Raider defense and made eleven 3s in a game that was tied at 68 after regulation. Brandone Francis matched a career high and led the Red Raiders with 17 points after going 7-for-12 with three 3-pointers, while Culver and Moretti had 15 points each. Mooney scored five of his 10 points in overtime, while freshman Kyler Edwards had 12 points after hitting two 3-pointers. Culver added nine rebounds and five assists and finished his sophomore season averaging 18.5 points, 6.4 rebounds, and 3.7 assists per game.

At halftime, Texas Tech trailed by only three points following a first half where the deficit had been as many as 10, after having led

Support for the Red Raiders reached its peak during the run through the NCAA tournament. From Tulsa to Anaheim to Minneapolis, the Red Raider hotels were swarmed by fans. Sendoffs before games became larger and larger as the team advanced and made the team feel like rock stars.

by as many as four. The Red Raiders were 5-for-12 from beyond the arc in the first half after starting the game 0-for-8 before a Moretti 3-pointer stopped a 7-0 run and cut the Cavaliers' lead to 9-6. Virginia had its biggest lead of the half at 17-7 on a pair of free throws before Francis and Edwards hit a pair of 3-pointers to cut it to 17-13. Another Francis 3-pointer followed by Moretti hitting a 3-pointer tied the game at 19 and the Red Raiders would take their first lead of the game at 23-21 on a pair of Edwards free throws. The Cavaliers took a three-point lead into halftime with Ty Jerome hitting a 3-pointer with two seconds on the clock.

Texas Tech's NCAA Tournament résumé ended with impressive wins over Northern Kentucky, Buffalo, Michigan, Gonzaga, and Michigan State. The program is now 76-31 under Beard, who completed his third season by leading the program to the pinnacle of the sport.

"We'll bounce back," Beard said. "In terms of Texas Tech basketball, we're not going anywhere. We'll be back in this tournament sooner than later, and we intend to be a part of college basketball as we build the program. I just told them I loved them. You know, our relationship is just getting started. I'll be at those guys' weddings one day and hopefully when their kids get born and do everything I can to talk them out of getting into coaching so they don't ever feel like this. You know, I just love those guys."

Tariq Owens screams out encouragement for his teammates from the sidelines in the national championship final. Owens, who was limited due to the injury suffered against Michigan State, still provided five rebounds and a blocked shot for the Red Raiders in the final.

TTU (3) vs. UVA (1)
Final Score: 77–85 (Overtime)
April 8, 2019 • Minneapolis, Minnesota

	FG	3-PT	Reb	Ast	Pts
Norense Odiase	1-1	0-0	6	0	5
Tariq Owens	1-3	0-1	5	0	3
Matt Mooney	4-9	2-6	1	3	10
Jarrett Culver	5-22	0-6	9	5	15
Davide Moretti	5-10	3-6	2	0	15
Brandone Francis	7-12	3-7	4	0	17
Deshawn Corprew	0-1	0-1	0	0	0
Kyler Edwards	4-5	2-3	3	1	12

The Virginia Cavaliers start against the Texas Tech Red Raiders in the 2019 NCAA Men's Final Four National Championship game at U.S Bank Stadium on April 8, 2019 in Minneapolis, Minnesota.
Photo by Jamie Schwaberow/NCAA Photos via Getty Images.

Texas Tech freshman Kyler Edwards drives to the basket against Virginia in the NCAA National Championship Final. Edwards finished the game with 12 points, including hitting two 3-pointers for the Red Raiders against the Cavaliers.

Brandone Francis led the Red Raiders with 17 points in the NCAA National Championship Final after hitting seven shots from the field, including three 3-pointers. Francis also added four rebounds in a game where he played 37 minutes as a reserve.

Davide Moretti buried a 3-pointer to cut Virginia's lead to 65–64 with 1:33 remaining as the Red Raiders fought back in the national championship game.

Texas Tech strength and conditioning coach John Reilly fires up the team during the Final Four.

Davide Moretti gets through the Virginia defense for two of his 15 points in the NCAA title game. Moretti hit three 3-pointers in the game and also had two steals.

Coach Beard talks to the team during a timeout against Virginia in the NCAA Championship Final.

Brandone Francis fights his way to the basket against Virginia's Ty Jerome.

Down six with four minutes to play, Matt Mooney drilled a 3-pointer to take the score to 56–59 as the Red Raiders started chipping away.

It was a painful day, but the Red Raiders were surrounded by support during a welcome-back event at the United Supermarkets Arena upon their arrival in Lubbock after the national championship game loss to Virginia. The ceremony included speeches from Chris Beard and Norense Odiase who both broke down as they expressed what the support from the Red Raider fans had meant to them throughout the season.

Norense Odiase gave an impassioned speech to an arena filled with supporters when the Red Raiders returned from Minnesota.

KEVIN HARLAN (TNT): "While watching the Red Raiders in their closed practice the day before their Sweet 16 game against Michigan, I was stunned by what I was witnessing. Players and coaches volleying all over the floor with energetic voices in constant motion practicing, teaching, applauding, then huddling. Over and over and over again. Bonding in the way champions bond. Supporting each other the way champions support. Exuding incredible confidence. Executing and preparing and practicing like it was the first of the season. Unbelievable energy orchestrated by this coach who had probably done it hundreds of times before, but with the passion on that March afternoon in California of the first time. It was then that I realized that what I had been hearing and reading about all these months was true. One of the most unique coaches in college basketball with a special group of players ranging from grad transfers to freshmen were a force that had to be seen to be appreciated. A team in full. Perhaps the truest example of a team that I've seen in over two decades broadcasting the NCAA Tournament. And I was struck by this — that regardless of where the journey of life takes each of them, each will remember their time and lessons learned with this team, and with that coach, and what was accomplished together as a team as they played for a national championship at the Final Four."

...covered one quite like this year's basketball team at Texas Tech. From the itinerant coach to his poor chief of staff to the defensive guru to the hometown kid turned lottery pick to the first Italian player in the Final Four to the two grad transfers ... the Red Raiders 2018–19 season reads more like a movie."

PART V:
THE LEGACY

From the Coach Beard Glossary:

Dreamers – At my press conference when I was hired here at Tech, I said that we were going to compete for the conference championship and to make the Final Four. A lot of people thought I was crazy, so I need to associate myself with people who dream like I do. The first step to doing anything special is having high expectations and a vision. Then you go to work. This year's team was on the same page. We thought from the first day that we could win the Big 12 championship and then for the national championship. This was a group of dreamers who worked to reach their dreams.

Texas Tech celebrated its historic season with a banquet inside the United Supermarkets Arena two weeks after the championship game. The team told stories from the season and enjoyed one final night together.

Chris Beard earned the Associated Press National Coach of the Year award after leading the Red Raiders to the Big 12 regular-season championship and the program's first Final Four appearance. He accepted the award prior to the start of the Final Four in Minneapolis, Minnesota.

AP COACH OF THE YEAR

MINNEAPOLIS (AP)—Chris Beard has never ventured far from the work, work, work approach that guided his career on its winding path through obscure, overlooked coaching jobs.

No reason to change it, not with Beard guiding Texas Tech to college basketball's biggest stage at the Final Four—and now recognition as the Associated Press men's college basketball coach of the year.

"I've always believed you have to be who you are," Beard said in an interview with the AP. "You can never forget who you are.... Sometimes as you advance in the profession and the logo on your shirt changes or the title next to your name changes, you kind of change. I've never wanted to do that."

Beard earned 20 of 64 votes from the same panel that selects the weekly AP Top 25, with voters submitting ballots before the start of the NCAA Tournament. Beard's team had won a share of its first Big 12 regular-season titles at the time of the voting. In the tournament, Texas Tech pushed past top-seeded Gonzaga to win the West and earn its ticket to Minneapolis.

Houston's Kelvin Sampson was second with 13 votes after the Cougars finished with a program-record 33 wins before losing in the Sweet 16.

Beard and Sampson were the only coaches to receive at least 10 votes, with 12 coaches splitting the rest of the ballots.

Not bad for a team that lost six of its top eight scorers from last year's Elite Eight run. Nor for a 46-year-old coach who is only in his third season at Texas Tech since making stops at Division II and III programs within the past seven years.

It's sheer force of will that helped Beard get here, a tireless work ethic rooted in the simple belief that anything less won't be enough,

Coach Beard with his daughters (from left) Avery, Ella, and Margo and his girlfriend, Randi Trew.

along with the feeling of being an underdog no matter how many games his team wins.

"It's just reality, it's not a made-up story," Beard said. "I wasn't a great Division I player myself and everything that I've kind of worked for in this has just been about trying to prove people wrong and constantly trying to validate our last success.

"Even this week with everything at stake, I find myself kind of thinking about next year and our recruiting class and starting next week," Beard said. "I don't think it's pressure, but I feel that responsibility to get back in the fight next year. That's just my mentality."

Now, Beard joins many other top coaches like John Wooden, Bill Self, and John Calipari with the AP award. In this Final Four, Tony Bennett of Virginia and Michigan State's Tom Izzo have also won the award.

"It's humbling, it's just kind of surreal when I look at the names of coaches," Beard said. "To be in that neighborhood has just always been a dream of mine....To me it's just kind of a team award. I really believe that everybody in my past is a big, big part of this as well."

Moretti talks about winning
the Elite 90 Award with Jim Nantz.

MORETTI EARNS ELITE 90 AWARD

TEXAS TECH sophomore Davide Moretti earned the Elite 90 winner for the 2019 NCAA Division I Men's Basketball Championship.

Moretti, majoring in human science, carried a 3.71 GPA. He was presented with the award at the championship banquet on Thursday night in Minnesota before the start of the Final Four. He was named an All-Big 12 Conference Third Team selection as one of the top shooters in the nation and went into the Final Four ranked second in the country by shooting 92.2 percent at the free-throw line where he was 95 or 103.

The ELITE 90, an award founded by the NCAA, recognizes the true essence of the student-athlete by honoring the individual who has reached the pinnacle of competition at the national championship level in his or her sport, while also achieving the highest academic standard among his or her peers. The Elite 90 is presented to the student-athlete with the highest cumulative grade-point average participating at the finals site for each of the NCAA's 90 championships.

Past Texas Tech recipients are Kim Kaufman from women's golf in the 2011-12 season, Montene Speight of women's track and field in 2014-15, and baseball's Tyler Floyd in 2015-16.

Eligible student-athletes are sophomores or above who have participated in their sport for at least two years with their school. They must be an active member of the team, traveling and a designated member of the squad size at the championship.

Moretti is presented the Elite 90 Award at the Final Four by NCAA President Mark Emmert.

Chris Beard was interviewed by CBS's Jim Nantz and addressed the crowd at the team's open practice the day before the start of the Final Four.

IN THE SPOTLIGHT

MEDIA ATTENTION was high throughout the season for the Red Raiders, but the run in the NCAA tournament significantly increased the spotlight on the basketball program and Texas Tech University. The Red Raiders were featured nationally on CBS, ESPN, NCAA.com, *Sports Illustrated,* CBSSports.com, *Time* magazine, ESPN Radio, NBC, ABC, *The Athletic,* *The Wall Street Journal,* Dan Patrick Show, the Associated Press, Yahoo! Sports, *USA Today,* and multiple other broadcasts and publications.

In terms of numbers, from March 14 to April 10, media exposure was at its peak with Texas Tech receiving 51,000 editorial mentions with a coverage reach of over 41 billion, according to a report by Meltwater. The coverage had an advertising value of $379 million during the run and a global reach of 76 countries.

On social media, more than 1,000 articles on the Texas Tech basketball program were shared three million times during the postseason run, and @TexasTechMBB led the nation with over 629,000 interactions during the NCAA tournament. Texas Tech played 23 of its games on ESPN networks, seven on Fox Sports, three on TNT, and four on CBS during its historic season.

Tariq Owens talks with the media during an open-locker room session during the NCAA Tournament.

Matt Mooney answers questions during an open-locker room session at the Final Four. The Red Raider locker room was open for 30 minutes during practice days in Minnesota and allowed the national media to interview every player and coach for stories about the team.

Holly Rowe interviews Jarrett Culver after winning against the University of Texas.

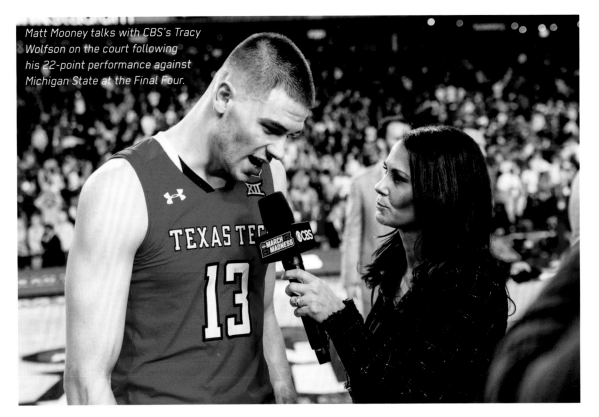

Matt Mooney talks with CBS's Tracy Wolfson on the court following his 22-point performance against Michigan State at the Final Four.

Chris Beard talks with the TNT crew of Kevin Harlan, Dana Jacobson, Reggie Miller, and Dan Bonner prior to the start of the Sweet 16 in Anaheim, California.

CULVER GETS DRAFTED

JARRETT CULVER'S SEASON was a lot like his team's. He began the season under-valued. He was considered a late first-round or early second-round pick. He ended the season as one of the most exciting prospects in college basketball. Even though he was the biggest star in Lubbock, Culver had a team-first attitude. In Coach Beard's game plan, he was as much an off-ball threat as he was an interior scorer. Culver did everything well.

There was nothing but love in the room as Jarrett Culver informed a full crowd of fans of his intention to declare for the NBA Draft. A hometown kid, Culver talked about growing up in Lubbock, living out a dream to play college basketball at the highest level, and the support that overwhelmed him from the Texas Tech fans for two seasons. On stage with him at the announcement, Coach Beard publicly endorsed the decision, while Culver's parents, brothers, and grandmother were all there to support him on his decision. On June 20, Culver was selected by the Minnesota Timberwolves with the sixth pick in the NBA Draft.

CARLOS SILVA (Lubbock Avalanche-Journal): "The chemistry among the players of the Texas Tech men's basketball team ensured a special season was in store. Chris Beard and his coaching staff are experts at bringing in talented players and getting all of them to mesh together and figure out their roles. Most important, though, was the Red Raiders' ability to continue to get better through an NCAA Tournament run that ended in the national title game. The foundation has been laid for future success and the Texas Tech faithful will have plenty to cheer for in the years to come inside United Supermarkets Arena."

Chris Beard is interviewed by Robert Giovannetti at the Final Four Media Day.

BRIAN HAMILTON (The Athletic): "What's so striking about Texas Tech is that they're always themselves, in every possible way, and how totally comfortable they are with that. Players, coaches, staff—there's no pretense or play-acting. It's a team that is incredibly invested but one that also just doesn't give a single rip what anyone else thinks. I can't blame them for it. Being who they are, without apology, made history."

THE SEASON IN NUMBERS & HONORS

- NCAA National Runner-Up

- Advanced to first Final Four in program history

- Reached Elite Eight for second straight season

- Big 12 Conference Regular-Season Co-Champion
  - New program wins record

- NCAA Tournament results
  - R1 Northern Kentucky (72-57)
  - R2 Buffalo (78-58)
  - Sweet 16 Michigan (63-44)
  - Elite Eight Gonzaga (75-69)
  - Final Four Michigan State (61-51)
  - National Championship Virginia (77-85 OT)

- NCAA Tournament record 5-1

- 14-4 record in Big 12 play
  - New program conference wins record

- 9-Game conference win streak
  - Longest Big 12 streak in program history

- 58-17 record the last two years
  - Best two-year stretch in program history

- Margin of victory
  - Won 23 games by double digits; 11 wins by 20 or more points; 6 wins by 30 or more

- Unranked in preseason polls
  - Finished No. 7 in AP Poll
  - No. 2 in USA Today Coaches Poll

- Picked 7th in preseason Big 12 poll
  - Won share of regular-season title with Kansas State

- First university from Texas to reach national championship game since Houston in 1984

- Fourth Texas school to advance to the national final

- 31-7 overall record

- Attendance
  - Averaged 12,098 fans per home game, which ranked second in the Big 12 and was 24th nationally
  - Had four sellouts and over 14,000 fans in seven games at the United Supermarkets Arena
  - Played in front of over 72,000 fans in both games at the Final Four in Minneapolis, Minnesota

- Defensive prowess
  - The Red Raiders led the nation in defensive efficiency in the Pomeroy Ratings and limited 20 opponents to under 60 points, 16 to below 35% shooting; six opponents shot under 30% and only six scored more than 70 points all season

- **Finished the season shooting 46.9% from the field, 36.5% on 3-pointers and 73.2% at the free-throw line**
    - Had nine games with 10 or more 3-pointers and five games with 20 or more free throws as a team
    - Had a season-high 16 3-pointers against Kansas and hit 30 free throws against Baylor
    - Hit nine 3-pointers in the Elite Eight against Gonzaga, nine against Michigan State in the Final Four semifinal and 10 in the national championship against Virginia

- **Chris Beard**
    - AP National Coach of the Year
    - Big 12 Coach of the Year
    - USBWA District Coach of the Year
    - Texas Association of Basketball Coaches Coach of the Year

- **Jarrett Culver**
    - Big 12 Player of the Year, Final Four All-Tournament Team
    - NCAA West Region Most Outstanding Player
    - John R. Wooden Award Finalist
    - AP All-America 2nd Team
    - USBWA All-America 2nd Team
    - Sporting News All-America 2nd Team
    - Final Four All-Tournament Team
    - Jerry West Award Finalist
    - All-Big 12 First-Team
    - NABC All-District
    - Big 12 All-Academic Team
    - NCAA West Region All-Tournament Team
    - 3-time Big 12 Player of the Week

- **Matt Mooney**
    - All-Big 12 Second Team
    - Final Four All-Tournament Team
    - All-Big 12 Newcomer Team
    - All-Big 12 Defensive Team

- **Davide Moretti**
    - All-Big 12 Third-Team
    - CoSIDA Academic All-District
    - Academic All-Big 12
    - NCAA Elite 90 Award

- **Tariq Owens**
    - Naismith Defensive Player of the Year Semifinalist
    - All-Big 12 Honorable Mention
    - All-Big 12 Defensive Team

- **Andrew Sorrells, Avery Benson, Parker Hicks, Norense Odiase, Malik Ondigo**
    - Academic All-Big 12

Coach Beard takes a moment to reflect between sessions at the Big 12 Media Day in Kansas City.

From unranked at the start of the season to the FINAL 4 & National Championship game, our 2018-19 team was special. All championship teams are. Our journey began in Stanton TX at a team retreat where we committed to standards of unselfishness, discipline, defense, & consistency. Six months later on a Saturday in Ames Iowa, we won our 9th consecutive BIG 12 game to capture the first BIG 12 championship in program history. In March Madness we re-committed as a team with a plan of: 1) Smell the Roses & 2) Be us. Together we executed this plan to near perfection before running out of time on the final Monday night. Thank you to the best fans in college basketball, Red Raider Nation. Thank you to our players & staff for your loyalty, sacrifice, & commitment to team basketball & winning. A special thank you to our seniors, my guys; Matt, Tariq, Brandone, & Norense for your trust & leadership.

C Beard
4:1

ACKNOWLEDGMENTS

WHEN THE CONFETTI fell for the final time on that Monday night in Minnesota and it was Virginia celebrating, and not us, the emotion in the locker room was overwhelming. As a communications staff, we stood in the back of the locker room as part of the basketball program. We weren't taking notes and our cameras were turned off. In that moment, we felt for the players and coaches who had let us into their lives all season and had taken us on a historic journey.

One of the treasures of a project like this is getting the opportunity to relive once-in-a-lifetime memories, but there are not any images in this book from the final meeting of the team in the locker room. That was an emotional moment that belonged to a group of guys who had come together in the summer, bonded at the team retreat, ran through a non-conference schedule, and made history by winning the conference championship and advancing to the national championship final.

In sports communication, a book like this would not be possible without the team you're covering embracing it. From the beginning, Coach Chris Beard, his staff, and the players understood that their journey was going to be special and that they were representing more than just themselves. The access that was granted to the Tech communications staff cannot be oversold. We traveled to the team retreat and slept in bunk beds, just like the coaches and players. We were with them at the first practice, at barbeque restaurants in Kansas City, on the beach in Miami, on the streets of New York, at Disneyland, and ultimately in that locker room in Minnesota after time had run out. We rode on the same planes, stayed at the same hotels, and took pride in capturing moments that connected the team and their fans. Chris Beard and his team embraced our role and not only invited us, but expected us, to be there for every step along the way.

Without the photographers who captured these iconic images, this book would not have been possible. The work of Norvelle Kennedy,

Elise Bressler, Matt Mika, Wes Peters, Evan Triplett, Elizabeth Hertel, Blake Zimmerman, Logan Hawk, Blake Silverthorn, Michael Strong, and Derrick Spencer helped fill the pages and bring forth memories that are sure to evoke emotion for all fans who were along for the amazing journey. Kennedy, who started shooting photos for Texas Tech Athletics in 1995, was there from the team photo in September to the final Monday night. He spent the season chronicling the Red Raiders at home and on the road, capturing images at practices, team dinners and adventures, and, of course, games. Kennedy continually produces high-quality images for Tech throughout the years and we cannot thank him enough. Along with Kennedy, an amazing group of student photographers has a passion for sports photography and storytelling that brought fans in throughout the season on social media, and their efforts jump off the pages within this book. Their work will keep the memories of our historic season alive forever and shows the talent that lives on the Texas Tech campus.

From Beard on, the basketball program let us into their lives throughout the season. We appreciate the coaching and support staff of Tim MacAllister, Liz Cope, Mark Adams, Brian Burg, Max Lefevre, Sean Sutton, Glynn Cyprien, Chris Williams, John Reilly, Colin Prentiss, Brandon Lee, Darryl Dora, Ronald Ross, Casey Perrin, Anthony Johnson, Taylor Sinclair, Matt Temple, Elliott De Wit, Gino Saucedo, Cooper Anderson, Colin Baxter, Brendan Baier, Jake Loy, Noah Parker, Cooper Burnett, and Dale Bryant who helped us throughout the season.

They played in high-pressure games throughout the year, but the players always embraced us and treated us like teammates. We appreciate Norense Odiase, Tariq Owens, Brandone Francis, Matt Mooney, Davide Moretti, Jarrett Culver, Andrew Sorrells, Kyler Edwards, Deshawn Corprew, Malik Ondigo, Avery Benson, Parker Hicks, and Josh Mballa for allowing us to be a part of an amazing journey with them. These student-athletes dedicated themselves throughout the season and provided us enough memories that we could have made this book a million pages.

The following individuals were also key to the production of this book: Robert Giovannetti, Drew Ingraham, Paige Holland, Kirby Hocutt, Tony Hernandez, Dusty Womble, Chris Level, Geoff Haxton, Jonathan Botros, and Justin Opperman. Their belief and support in storytelling allowed us to have multiple photographers and videographers at games and on trips throughout the season. Thanks also to Hannah Gaskamp, Christie Perlmutter, Travis Snyder, and everyone at TTU Press. Everyone valued our work in communications, and we are grateful for the opportunity to produce this collection.

There are countless individuals who came together to help tell the story of a team that began the season unranked and reached the national championship final, but this book would not have been produced without the support of the Red Raider nation. The passion that Texas Tech fans showed throughout the year at games and on social media was overwhelming. There was never a time when the team felt alone or unsupported, and our athletic communications department dedicated itself to feed the fans with the content they desired. Books like this are not produced after every season, but not every season captures a fan base like this team did.

Fans fell in love with the players and coaches on a deeper level, and we built this book to keep the memories alive forever.

Wes Bloomquist

INDEX